Observation and its Application to Social Work

of related interest

Competence in Social Work Practice
Edited by Kieran O'Hagan
ISBN 1 85302 332 9

Handbook of Theory for Practice Teachers in Social Work
Edited by Joyce Lishman
ISBN 1 85302 098 2

Learning and Teaching in Social Work:
Towards Reflective Practice
Edited by Margaret Yelloly and Mary Henkel
ISBN 1 85302 237 3

Learning Through Child Observation
Mary Fawcett
ISBN 1 85302 288 8

Staff Supervision in a Turbulent Environment
Lynette Hughes and Paul Pengelly
ISBN 1 85302 327 2

Observation and its Application to Social Work

Rather Like Breathing

Edited by Pat Le Riche and Karen Tanner

Jessica Kingsley Publishers
London and Philadelphia

First published in the United Kingdom in 1998
by Jessica Kingsley Publishers Ltd,
116 Pentonville Road,
London N1 9JB, England
and
325 Chestnut Street, Philadelphia,
PA 19106, USA.

Copyright 1998 Jessica Kingsley Publishers

Library of Congress Cataloging in Publication Data
A CIP catalogue record for this book is available from the Library of Congress

British Library Cataloguing in Publication Data

ISBN 1 85302 629 8 hb
ISBN 1 85302 630 1 pb

Printed and Bound in Great Britain by
Athenaeum Press, Gateshead, Tyne and Wear

Contents

Figures

For Jeremy, Lottie and Maudie,
Ted and Nick

Acknowledgements

Among the many people who have helped us, directly or indirectly, in writing this book, we would like particularly to thank the following:

Our authors for their commitment to this book. During the process of writing the book the authors met to discuss their ideas about observation. These meetings were lively, stretching and supportive. We thank the authors for the time and energy they gave generously to these meetings. The subsequent chapters make a significant contribution to developing and extending ideas about observation.

Goldsmiths' MA/Diploma in Social Work students for their lively participation in the observation sequence – their curiosity and debates were an important influence in developing this book. In particular, we would like to thank the students who gave kind permission for their observation experiences to be cited.

The families who kindly gave permission for their lives to be observed and from whom so much has been learnt.

Cherry Rowlings, Danielle Turney and Walter Finn for help at different stages in the process.

Vivienne Rose for her help in putting the book together and robust support.

Thanks to Jo Campling for her encouragement at the early stage of the book and to Helen Parry for her editorial support.

Introduction

Karen Tanner

The Context of the Book

This book is about observation and its application to social work education and practice. The aim of the book is to draw attention to the place and value of observation within social work. In the process, the book analyses the multi-dimensional nature of observation and grounds the ideas generated through direct application in both practice and educational settings.

The development of the ideas in this book can usefully be conceptualised via the metaphor of a journey. In this introduction I will identify some of the stages in this journey which have been significant for me. However, this volume also charts the journey of a collection of people who, in various ways, work with observation in their professional lives. They have contributed their diverse experiences in their chapters. Although our experiences are different, we share an interest in exploring the terrain and horizon of this, so far undeveloped, aspect of social work.

The starting point of the journey was the initiative of the Central Council for Education and Training in Social Work (CCETSW) and the Tavistock Clinic to provide infant and child observation training for social work tutors and practitioners. This initiative was a response to a series of inquiries into the deaths of children (Blom-Cooper 1985; Blom-Cooper, Harding and MacMilton 1987; London Borough of Lambeth 1987) and the events in Cleveland in 1987 (Butler-Sloss 1988). Among the many concerns identified by the investigations were the professional failure to keep the child 'in mind' whilst working with the whole family, insufficient understanding of child development and the need to improve the quality of assessment skills.

Observation has long been recognised as a valuable component of many professional training programmes for work with young children – teaching, child psychotherapy and nursery workers, for example. However, it was not a feature of social work training. The CCETSW/Tavistock initiative was premised on the view that the incorporation of infant and child observation into social work education and practice would make an important contribution to the areas of professional knowledge and skill identified as inadequate by the inquiries.

As part of this development, I undertook an observation of a young child on the course at the Tavistock Clinic designed for social work tutors and practitioners. Subsequently, I undertook two further extensive observations. This experience has informed the way in which I have developed, with colleagues, an infant and child observation sequence as part of the Diploma in Social Work (DipSW) programme at Goldsmiths College.

The Tavistock Model of Observation

The observation programme for social workers developed by Judith Trowell and Gillian Miles (1991a, 1991b) at the Tavistock Clinic drew upon the Tavistock Model of infant and child observation originally devised by Esther Bick (1964). The Tavistock Model is informed by psychoanalytic ideas, most notably those of Melanie Klein and Wilfred Bion, and has a long tradition in professional training at the Tavistock Clinic. Although there has been an uneasy relationship between social work and psychoanalytic ideas since the 1970s, Trowell and Miles recognised that the aims of the Tavistock Model and its methodology were not entirely antithetical to social work. They therefore pioneered the application of the Tavistock's ideas about infant and child observation into the social work context. Whilst there have always been a number of different approaches to observation in the natural and social sciences, it is important to explore the Tavistock's model here as it has been highly influential and provides a context for the discussion which follows in this book.

The Tavistock Clinic introduced the idea of observational studies because of a concern to complement the theoretical training of child psychotherapists with direct and sustained close contact with a child. It was argued that observation would 'give each student a unique opportunity to observe the development of an infant more or less from birth in his home setting and in his relations to his immediate family and thus to find out for himself how these relationships emerge and develop' (Bick 1964, p.558). Here an important distinction is made between learning from experience and learning about things (Bion 1962). In transferring this idea to the social work context, social workers would be able to ground their knowledge of children in direct experience. This would enable a more sensitive and critically informed use of theoretical knowledge and procedures in the practice context. It would develop practitioners' skills in observation and the capacity to remain focused on the child whilst engaged with all the events taking place in the observation. Sustained contact with small children would also assist social workers to revise and develop more child-focused communication skills, including a recognition of the importance of play as a medium of communication. In addition, the process of observation equips social workers with the skills and qualities necessary for informed measured assessment. Such skills include a recognition of patterns of interaction, processes of communication and an ability to manage conflict. Social workers also need the personal qualities of tolerating uncertainty and avoiding premature judgement. Here it is necessary to move on to look at the methodological approach of the Tavistock Model and explore its contribution in developing these desired qualities.

Methodologically, the Tavistock's approach makes particular requirements of the observer role. The observer is not an active participant and, at the same time, the impossibility of being a fly on the wall is recognised. Although refraining from active participation, the observer is required to be mentally and emotionally engaged with the events and processes taking place in the observation. Observation within this model is more than simply looking. It is considerably more complex and requires the observer to be emotionally receptive, taking in and holding in the mind the physical and emotional experiences of the baby and her family and attempting to give some meaning to these experiences. In this process of constructing meaning attention is also given to the relationship between the observer and the family. Thinking about the unconscious emotional transactions taking place between the observer and the family is an important source of information about what is happening in the observation. In essence, this conceptualisation of the observer role is akin to Bion's (1962) idea of reverie, the state of mind required by parents to process and respond appropriately to their baby's primitive emotional communications (Margaret Rustin 1989). Within the social work context, Trowell and Miles (1991b) recognised significant parallels between the stance required of the observer and the approach required of social workers when responding to complex and uncertain problems:

> Although difficult and often puzzling, if students can be helped to distinguish the observation aspect of social work from the role of the active helpful social worker who intervenes, they will become clearer about their tasks of assessing, understanding and monitoring before acting. This capacity to reflect and think before acting is an invaluable

skill that comes out of observation training... Not acting but staying with the experience, and struggling to be clear about what you know and what remains unknown, is difficult. (p.133–4)

In addition to the specific stance of the observer, there are a number of other methodological requirements of the model. In terms of structure, the observer visits the family for one hour a week, on the same day each week, for a significant period of time – this can range between ten weeks and two years. This structure aims to provide the experience of building a detailed picture of a child's world and her development as it emerges over time.

Each hourly observation is recorded. However, as note taking detracts from the focus and engagement required of the observer, the recording takes place after the observation has occurred. In the written record of the observation, the observer aims to describe the moment-by-moment account of the observation in its raw state, that is in language free of premature theoretical conceptualisation. This approach discourages the influence of preconceptions and enables the observation to be registered in all its complexity before being codified (Michael Rustin 1989). It also facilitates a depth of learning as it enables other people to lend their perspective to the observation material.

Critical to the process of observation in the Tavistock's model is a structured space for reflection. In this approach, observers participate in small facilitated seminar groups and rotate presenting observations for discussion. There is a coming together of minds to digest and reflect upon the observation. The seminar also has an associated function of containment (Bion 1962) as it is a place where anxieties and uncertainty generated by the observation can be shared and thought about. Observation frequently arouses emotional responses in observers. These responses can be related to emotional communications taking place within the family or may be related to personal experiences of the observer. The containing and thinking aspect of the seminar is important in helping observers to distinguish the source of the feelings and to manage the sometimes overwhelming nature of the experience.

Trowell and Miles' pioneering work has had a notable influence within social work education and practice. A number of social work educators have recognised the value of incorporating infant and child observation into programmes of professional development at both the qualifying and post-qualifying levels and have used the Tavistock's model as an informing framework (McMahon and Farnfield 1994; Miles and Bridge 1997; Wilson

1992). Similarly, the value of developing observation practice within children and families social work is growing. The Department of Health (1988) guidance on assessment clearly states the place of observation within the assessment process.

The Wider Application of Ideas about Observation

As infant and child observation has become established as an important vehicle for enhancing the quality of social work with children and families, so interest has been stimulated about its application to other aspects of social work practice. This represents the next significant stage in this book. Infant and child observation was influential in shaping the ideas and understanding of many of the contributors. However, curiosity and creative imagination has led to the development and application of these early ideas to a range of social work settings. In this book, contributors share their experiences in applying observation in a psychiatric unit, management practice, staff consultancy in residential children's homes, practice teaching and practice assessing, multi-disciplinary post-qualifying education for health and welfare professionals and in the context of family therapy. In this process of extending the application of observation, the learning generated has been deepened and rich new seams of learning discovered. Within this book discussions take place about the relationship between observation and the development of the reflective practitioner, currently a conceptualisation of social work which is attracting much attention in these times of marketisation and competency. Observation is also identified as having an important role in recognising and modifying socially structured defences within organisations. Similarly, there are discussions of observation in the context of power relations and anti-oppressive practice. These are examples of some of the important social work issues to which observation is making a contribution. As observation is a developing concept, it follows that other areas could have been discussed – observation and social work research and observation and child protection are two examples. However, the range of discussion in this book makes a contribution to continuing debates about the development of observation within social work education and practice.

The Application of a Power Lens to Observation

This book makes clear that the debates about observation involve a number of different theoretical ways of thinking about observation and these differences are shaped by a range of epistemological traditions. While the Tavistock's ideas remain influential, the contributors explore the impact of material from a number of other disciplines – such as ethnography, psychology and critical social policy on observation and social work. However, with the exception of Mark Baldwin's (1994) work, observation has not taken sufficient account of power relations and anti-oppressive practice, from whichever perspective it is approached. As Pat Le Riche and I have continued to work with issues of observation, this absence of a power perspective has become more central to our thinking. This has developed through personal experience of observation, discussion with student observers and our work in developing ideas about hierarchies of power within observation in the practice context (Tanner and Le Riche 1995). An important staging post in the book's journey, therefore, has been to incorporate a perspective on power relations within observation. Observation will be strengthened as a social work tool if it is able to complement the rich learning generated through the focus on the individual with an informed understanding of the impact and pervasiveness of power relations in all their dimensions. The observation process needs to link micro and macro issues.

Chapters One and Two provide a context for the application of ideas about observation in the chapters that follow. Chapter One discusses the characteristic and dimensions of observation and describes the influence of the scientific and narrative traditions. The influence of observation on debates about competence and reflective practice is also discussed. Chapter Two develops the discussion by arguing that if observation is to be congruent with the theoretical constructs, values and legislation informing social work practice, it needs to develop a power perspective. The Equality Model of observation is described and discussed in an attempt to redress this incongruity. Subsequently, all of the chapters in this book explore the issue of power and anti-oppressive practice, albeit in separate and different ways. Some of the contributors address the issue in relation to the process of observation, for example Patricia Kearney, John Simmonds and Kate Leonard. Other chapters, written by Marilyn Miller-Pietroni, Hazelanne Lewis and Moira Doolan, focus on the contribution of observation in counteracting oppressive and dehumanising practices. Together, we hope the discussions in this book can develop the power perspective in the observation dialogue. For all of us, the dialogue is still in progress and we hope it is in the spirit of debate that the reader will engage with the ideas expressed here.

References

Baldwin, M. (1994) 'Why observe children?' *Social Work Education 13*, 2, 74–85.

Bick, E. (1964) 'Notes on infant observation in psychoanalytic training.' *International Journal of Psychoanalysis 45*, 558–566.

Bion, W. (1962) *Learning from Experience.* London: Heinemann.

Blom-Cooper, L. (1985) *A Child in Trust.* London: London Borough of Brent.

Blom-Cooper, L., Harding, J. and MacMilton, E. (1987) *A Child in Mind.* London: London Borough of Greenwich.

Butler-Sloss, Lord Justice. (1988) *Report of the Inquiry into Child Abuse in Cleveland in 1987.* London: HMSO.

Department of Health (DoH) (1988) *Protecting Children. A Guide for Social Workers Undertaking a Comprehensive Assessment.* London: HMSO.

London Borough of Lambeth (1987) *Whose Child?* London: London Borough of Lambeth.

McMahon, L. and Farnfield, S. (1994) 'Infant and child observation as preparation for social work practice.' *Social Work Education 13*, 3, 81–98.

Miles, G. and Bridge, G. (1997) *On the Outside Looking In.* London: CCETSW.

Rustin, Margaret. (1989) 'Encountering primitive anxieties.' In L. Miller, M. Rustin, M. Rustin and J. Shuttleworth (eds) *Closely Observed Infants.* London: Duckworth Press.

Rustin, Michael. (1989) 'Observing infants: reflections on methods.' In L. Miller, M. Rustin, M. Rustin and J. Shuttleworth (eds) *Closely Observed Infants.* London: Duckworth Press.

Tanner, K. and Le Riche, P. (1995) '"You see but you do not observe." The art of observation and its application to practice teaching.' *Issues in Social Work Education 15*, 2, 66–80.

Trowell, J. and Miles, G. (1991a) 'The contribution of observation training to professional development in social work.' *Journal of Social Work Practice 5*, 1, 51–60.

Trowell, J. and Miles, G. (1991b) 'The place of an introduction to young child observation in social work training.' The Teaching of Child Care in the Diploma in Social Work: Guidance Notes for Programme Planners. London: CCETSW.

Wilson, K. (1992) 'The place of child observation in social work training.' *Journal of Social Work Practice 6*, 1, 37–47.

CHAPTER ONE

The Dimensions of Observation
Objective Reality or Subjective Interpretation
Pat Le Riche

Observation is in some ways rather like breathing: Life depends on it and we do it all the time, usually without reflection. The observation skills of watching, listening, counting and identifying patterns of social interaction are processes we tend to take for granted though we would, quite literally, be lost without them. (Peberdy 1993, p.47)

In this chapter I aim to develop a greater understanding of the characteristics of observation. This complex and multi-layered concept has not been fully developed in current social work literature where common understanding of observation is frequently assumed. One example of this is provided by the Central Council for Education and Training in Social Work (CCETSW) (1995) in its revision of the Diploma in Social Work Regulations: they require all student social workers to be directly observed during their practice placement on at least three occasions. In spite of the importance given to observation in those regulations, to date no operational definitions or guidelines have been produced. There appears to be little consensus about the meaning, purpose and use of direct observation in social work training. Similarly, in social work literature there is a growing recognition of the place of observation in practice, particularly in relation to work with children and families (Briggs 1995; Trowell and Miles 1991; Wilson 1992). 'The recognition that observation is a valuable training tool grew out of training involving intensive work with children. However, it is now thought to be useful for anyone in the caring professions having face-to-face contact with clients or supervising such work' (Trowell and Miles 1991, p.131). The starting point of this literature is the presumption of a shared understanding of the concept of observation, defined by its characteristics in action.

In contrast, in this chapter I will argue that observation is a contested and multi-dimensional concept which requires further analysis and greater precision in its use if it is to become a more effective tool of social work education and practice.

Some Characteristics of Observation

The Observation Continuum

At its simplest, the act of observation is part of the process of looking, seeing and understanding reality. Observation is also a universal activity which is continuous and characterised by passivity and lack of involvement. The emphasis, both in common sense terms and in dictionary definitions, is upon the use of the eyes and, subsequently, in comprehending what is seen. For most people, observation gives primacy to the truth of the visual, which predominates over the evidence of hearing, touch and smell (Reissman 1993).

These everyday characteristics provide a helpful starting point in thinking about the nature of observation since they enable us to explore the complex nature of the process of seeing. We should consider whether emphasis on visual activity is sufficient or whether ideas about observation need to take into account a broader range of characteristics and concerns.

Weade and Evertson (1991), in their work on the training of teachers, contrast 'ordinary' perception which emphasises the centrality of sensory processes to more formal, intentional and systematic observations which are 'used as a tool for obtaining evidence to answer a question or to make decisions that will affect others' (p.38). Adapting the ideas of Evertson and Green (1986), Weade and Evertson characterise these different forms of observation as a continuum with everyday perception at one end and formal, intentional action at the other. The point at which observations are placed on this continuum is affected by the movement of observation from a relatively simple sensory process at one end of the continuum to more formal, structured observation at the other. Relating this to social work, a practice teacher working with a student on placement may observe the student in a number of different situations, including in the team room and in semi-social interactions. The practice teacher will absorb the information gained during these observations but may not want to make use of them in the practice teacher role. However, the CCETSW regulations (1995) also require the practice teacher to arrange to observe the student on three occasions during the placement. These planned and formal observations introduce a second dimension into Weade and Evertson's model since they argue that the nature of observation is also characterised by the degree of 'intentionality' of the observer. In the practice teaching example, observations are planned and 'intentional' and lead to action both in terms of feedback as a significant part of the social work student's learning and also as part of the evidence for the assessment which influences decisions about the student's level of professional competence. This is in contrast to the tacit or informal observations which are associated with informal processes.

These informal ('tacit') and formal ('intentional') processes of observation are not mutually exclusive.

> When individuals take on roles as systematic, intentional observers, they do not cease to function as tacit observers of everyday events. Instead, all forms of observation might occur simultaneously. When observation is viewed as a form of systematic, intentional action, it is both similar (to) and different from ordinary tacit observation. The differences are primarily a function of emphasis and selection of a focus for observing. (Weade and Evertson 1991, p.38)

Thus perceptual and other sensory information gained by means of tacit observation does not necessarily result in action but it is always an element which is present during intentional observations. This would seem to imply that observation does not simply move through a continuum as a linear process but can also provide a feedback loop with information from formal and informal observations interacting together to inform the picture of the world around us.

The third dimension in Weade and Evertson's model consists of the influence of the situation chosen for the observation. An observer can choose to observe everyday events (social interactions), specific, chosen events (interacting with the team) or planned interactions (the contracted assessment during the placement). Weade and Evertson conclude '…the figure suggests an integration of relationships along three dimensions: the degree of formality chosen, the observer's level of intentionality, and the nature of the occasion for observing. Each influences what will occur and how it will occur' (Weade and Evertson 1991, p.38).

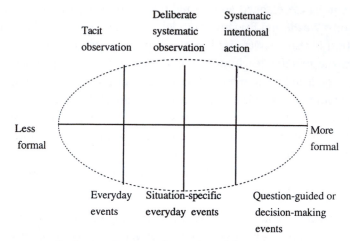

Figure 1.1: Individual as observer and actor in social settings
Source: *Weade and Evertson 1991, p.38.*

The Vertical Axis

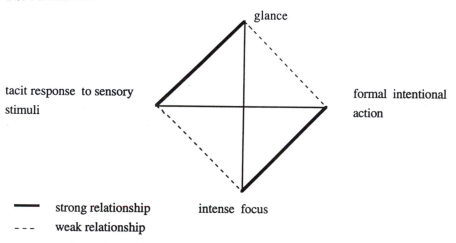

Figure 1.2: Observation matrix

The vertical axis introduced in Figure 1.2 suggests an additional qualitative dimension influencing the character of observation. On this vertical axis, observation moves from a superficial activity (the glance) to the intense focus which is necessary for effective, intentional observation so that the complex material available is both noted and understood. This matrix suggests ways in which different points on the vertical and horizontal axes can be connected. There are more likely to be strong connections at the points suggested in Figure 1.2. Thus the 'glance' is more likely to be a characteristic of informal observation while an 'intensive focus' is necessary in a planned observation which could result in action. The most obvious example of this form of observation in social work practice is its use for assessment, but in the social work literature in general, discussion of observation most frequently relates to the intentional and formal definition of observation.

Having begun to explore some of the complexities of observation, I now wish to broaden my discussion to examine a number of other relevant dimensions of the concept.

As ideas about observation are often discussed uncritically, I concentrate on three further issues: the time dimension, the role of the observer and whether observation attempts to be holistic or selective. In doing this I will suggest that rather than being a normative concept, the characteristics of observation are both paradoxical and conflictual.

The Time Dimension

Observation is influenced by the dimension of time in a number of different ways. Time has an historical imperative which has influenced the way in which observation is understood and used. A hundred years ago, observation would have been influenced by the prevailing scientific and rational paradigm of knowledge. Ideas about observation continue to be responsive to paradigm shifts taking place over time. For example, it is possible to chart different ideas about observation which have taken account of the growth of social science knowledge which has taken place during this century. These ideas will be developed later in this chapter.

A chronological time perspective influences both the shape and character of the observation. Along this dimension observation can take place longitudinally as an ongoing process or it can be a snapshot captured in a moment of time. This snapshot has the potential to provide a picture of the situation in all its complexity while a longitudinal perspective facilitates access to patterns and changes in relationships, individual behaviours and group dynamics over time. This linear perspective further emphasises the different purposes of observation.

A recognition of the subjective dimension of time further informs our understanding of observation. Being aware of this subjective dimension enables us to recognise that individuals experience time differently. For

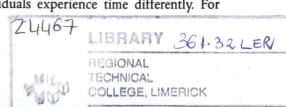

instance, taking a life-cycle perspective, small children have little internalised concept of measured time. Adolescents appear to experience time rushing by while for older people time seems to be a more complex experience. This complexity is encapsulated by Margery Fry (1966):

> When I know that my years are few I want to live them fully, to make up for the waste of neglected experience. But time plays us a dirty trick. With my retarded metabolism the days and weeks seem to race by, and even the number of hours in the day which I have the energy to use profitably grow fewer. Yet though time on a large scale is so short, from hour to hour the minutes seem to drag. (p.10)

Similarly, these characteristics need to be borne in mind when considering the impact of subjective time on the observer during the process of the observation. This could affect the observer's capacity to sustain the role for the period of the observation, tolerate the issues that arise and also influence the ability to pay detailed attention to the material: '...how boring it is to spend an hour watching children on the playground for more than one day. 60 minutes never seemed so long' (Sommer and Sommer, quoted in Pope and Gilbert 1984, p.32).

Apart from these chronological and subjective dimensions of time, the nature of observation is also shaped by an understanding of time as a resource. In this sense, time is 'spent' and 'used' during the process of observing. Later in this chapter I will discuss the ways in which a range of sampling techniques can be used to structure observation, controlling both the data and the available time (Fawcett 1996). In this sense, all these dimensions of time have to be recognised as significant influences affecting the character and process of observation.

Selective or Holistic Observation

It is also important to recognise the dimension of selectivity when considering the characteristics of observation. Observation which has a specific focus will involve the observer in selecting particular aspects of the material generated. This type of observation may be used when seeking evidence of a child's attachment to a carer.

> The difficulty in developing skills in this area (assessment of attachment) of child protection work is evident, and the cumulative experiences of the observation provide a valuable opportunity for doing

this. I therefore introduced the observation sequence with a day workshop and guided reading on attachment theory, and students are
asked as part of their reflections on the observations to consider the
evidence of attachment and attachment behaviour. (Wilson 1992,
pp.39–40)

Similarly, it may apply when a practice teacher is looking for evidence of a
particular piece of knowledge, skills or value in action. Alternatively,
observation can attempt to achieve as complete a picture as possible of what
has occurred during the period of the observation – for example young child
observation (Trowell and Miles 1991). However, in both these situations
attention needs to be given to the 'filter' which determines the observer's
selection of evidence or holistic representation. Whether the observation is
selective or holistic, the filter which determines the material to be selected
can never be neutral. When an observer is selecting material according to a
predetermined format, it is the structure which acts as a filter identifying for
the observer what is considered worthy of note and what is excluded. In an
holistic observation the filter will be the product of the interests, prejudices
and feelings of the observer. The observer's holistic representation of an
event will consciously or unconsciously reflect personal preoccupations (e.g.
gender) since 'I am always looking at the world through some perspective
and I can never get outside this perspective so as to test it' (Dean 1989).

The Observer and the Observed

The position of the observer in relation to what is being observed remains a
contested issue and I will address three particular dichotomies. The first of
these relates to ideas about the boundary of the observation and whether the
observer is.inside or outside that boundary. Second, we need to take account
of the observer's relationship to the material generated by the observation.
Third, we also have to consider whether the observer is involved in a
subjective or objective process.

Some models of observation suggest that the observer should attempt to
locate herself outside the situation that is being observed. The ideal is to
maintain distance in order to retain the freshness and neutrality of the
outsider role. This view has, in the past, been associated with ethnographic
accounts of research into cultures where the advantages of being an outsider
have been described and analysed (Parlett 1984). Similarly, this neutrality

and distance have been regarded as essential components in the effective use of observation in the natural sciences.

For others, there is an inevitability about the observer becoming part of the process, though the nature and degree of this involvement may vary. For example, when families are being observed, some observers, like Briggs (1995), describe a process of involvement characterised by physical inactivity but emotional and intellectual engagement. Briggs argues that:

> the observer's role is not that of the fly on the wall, although re-
> quired to refrain from initiating activity and interaction, he (sic) is
> expected to maintain a friendly and receptive attitude to the family,
> of whom he is a privileged guest. He is also expected to be active
> emotionally and mentally, and the observation of the events in the
> family is coupled with digesting the emotional impact of the en-
> counter. It is in any event not possible to be an observer in a family
> and go unnoticed, or to have no impact on the family system. Think-
> ing about the quality of this impact, in both directions, that is, on
> both the observer and the observed is an important part of the pro-
> cess of understanding the observational material. (p.105)

Parallel considerations exist in relation to the nature of the material generated by the observation. For some, the product of the observation will consist entirely of the 'hard' data seen, quantified and recorded. No attention will be paid to extraneous or personal information. The process of the observation is similarly not significant; observation is an event not a process. In an alternative view of the constituents of an observation, Briggs argues that thinking about the impact of the observation and paying attention to the thoughts and emotions generated inside the observer is an important part of the observation and contributes to understanding the observational material. In this paradigm the observer needs to understand and make use of thoughts and feelings generated by the experience as they are an important source of information. An example is provided by Fairhurst (1990), describing a piece of ethnographic research she undertook in a geriatric unit, where she emphasises the need to use the painful and uncomfortable feelings generated during her observations as a way of informing her understanding of both the process and the outcome of her work.

The questions underpinning these paradoxical views are linked to whether observations can or should be 'objective'. Is the ideal one in which the observer should strive for neutrality and objectivity or can the observer recognise, value and work with the subjective element of observation? In my view these questions are fundamental and before I can go any further in analysing and debating ideas about the nature of observation I need to examine further the epistemology underlying these different perspectives. I have argued elsewhere that two broad epistemological strands which I have characterised as 'scientific' and 'narrative' have influenced the development of models of observation (Le Riche and Tanner 1996). I will now go on to discuss these strands in greater detail.

'Scientific' Model of Observation

The first model of observation, which, in an earlier article, was described as scientific, has its origins in theories of knowledge which give priority to characteristics such as objectivity, rationality and accuracy of measurement (Le Riche and Tanner 1996). Within this epistemological tradition observation is most frequently regarded as a tool. For example, in a discussion of contrasting theories of knowledge, Henkel (1995) describes the development of ideas within the Cartesian paradigm with its concern 'to establish how the individual knowing subject could appreciate an external reality' (p.69). In this search for laws which could offer a coherent picture of this external world observation was a central tool. Similarly, Pope and Gilbert (1984) describe the use of observation in educational research as 'a primary tool within scientific enquiry'. '[It] is our basic method of getting information about the world about us...' (p.33). Briggs (1995) argues that observation has a significant part to play in the educational process: '[it has] emerged as a flexible tool for teaching and learning, where the original method has been demonstrably capable of adapting to different settings, time scales and consumer groups' (p.106).

Within the positivist approach to theory building, observation occupied a central position as the most significant means of collecting, validating and replicating information. 'Science was, above all else, an empirical activity and its base lay in the observation of what we can term "brute data": that is data which (are) not the result of judgement, interpretation, or other kinds of subjective mental operation' (Hughes 1980, p.36). As the development of natural science continued throughout the nineteenth and twentieth centuries, observation became equally important within the human sciences where scientific methods and epistemologies were influential. 'Most social scientists were agreed that the social sciences should model themselves on the natural sciences' (Hughes 1980, p.35). For example, in 1981 Barton and

Ascione reviewed a range of journal articles in behavioural psychology. They found that direct observation was an element of the methodology in 70 per cent of the research reported. Similarly, ethnographers have recognised the value of using observation and discussed its significance as a means of data collection (Hammersley and Atkinson 1983; Peberdy 1993). However, having been used initially in the natural sciences, this example demonstrates that direct observation had become centrally important to the development of other disciplines whether it was used as a means of understanding the natural world or building up a picture of a range of behaviour.

Within both the natural and human sciences, the scientific model of observation has common characteristics. In this approach, the aim was to collect data which were valid, reliable and designed to test the validity of hypotheses by repeated experimentation. In order to achieve these ideals, attention needed to be paid to the role of the observer. As far as possible, the stance of the observer had to be that of a detached non-participant – although, as Briggs (1993) points out, this 'objectivity' is a state which it is possible to strive for but may not be so easy to achieve. Quoting Kuhn, he argues that 'no scientific work is theory free' and is, therefore, affected by both the value position of the observer and the social structures within which the observation is taking place. However, Briggs suggests that the role of the observer changes across a spectrum:

> At one end of the spectrum is the wish to be removed from the action, to be as it were a 'fly on the wall', ideas which most closely relate to 'empirical realism'. At the other end of this spectrum the observer wants to be involved and therefore equal attention has to be given to the observer, the observation and the relationship between the two in the development of theory and practice. (p.1)

In order to achieve reliability in the collection and interpretation of data, recent accounts of observation within the scientific model have emphasised the training of observers in order to enable them to achieve accuracy, consistency and the optimum level of objectivity. In an account of the observation of classroom interactions, Flanders (1984) argues that the trained observer researching this area needs to act 'like an automatic device, albeit highly discriminating, [who] codes without hesitation at the instant an event is recognised' (p.64). This may be an extreme picture of the observer as a mechanical instrument but it encapsulates one view of the role and function of the observer within the scientific model.

As this example from Flanders implies, the scientific model requires the observer to record while the observation is taking place. As with all forms of data collection, for whatever purpose, ways have to be found to control and manage the volume of material generated. In many forms of scientific enquiry no attempt is made to observe everything, since the complexity of the resulting data would make it far more difficult to replicate. One way of resolving this problem is to observe specific aspects of behaviour rather than the broad sweep. Breaking down behaviour into smaller elements makes it easier to control and, in some situations, easier to change. The issue of controlling data becomes particularly significant when large-scale surveys or research projects are being undertaken. In this situation the behaviour being observed can be sampled rather than recorded in its entirety. Fawcett (1996) describes three main methods of sampling: event, activity and time sampling. Each of these requires the observer to focus on behaviour either at identified intervals of time or when specified events or activities are taking place. The resulting material is usually recorded by means of charts, codes or symbols rather than narrative accounts since, within positivist approaches, the aim is to achieve 'theoretically neutral observation language' (Hughes 1980, p.36). This has proved to be a complex issue within the human sciences (for further discussion of these points see Dearden 1979; Fawcett 1996; Rustin 1991).

Apart from the search for specific and definite findings, observation within this scientific model has a number of other characteristics. There is a greater emphasis on the observation of public events and behaviour rather than an interest in the private and personal (Rustin 1989). This model is also more likely to adopt a 'snapshot' approach to the behaviour observed rather than focus on a developmental approach to observing behaviour over time. However, both these points could be seen as generalisations since a number of authors have begun to look at the convergence between different epistemological approaches (Briggs 1993; Rustin 1989, 1991). In moving on to look at the characteristics of observation within the narrative model, we have to bear in mind the increasing scepticism about the feasibility of an objective search for reality and an awareness of the need to be 'wary of an idealised view of natural scientific method…' (Rustin 1991, p.135).

The Narrative Model of Observation

I use the term 'narrative' to describe a model which is influenced by very different ideas about the nature of knowledge. Narrative observation reflects a range of epistemologies which reject the Cartesian position of the rational individual contemplating objective reality (Henkel 1995). Within this broad tradition, positivist assumptions of neutrality and objectivity are challenged and, in consequence, the claim that legitimacy can only be conferred on knowledge produced in conditions of empirical 'scientific' enquiry is subject to radical critique. The claim that knowledge always exists within a context (Featherstone and Fawcett 1995) has led to an interest in the complex relationships between knowledge and the knower. Post-positivist thinking (Rossiter 1996) is characterised by, among others, ideas about subjectivity and context. The application of this thinking to observational studies has produced a conceptually different model of observation.

I would include within the post-positivist framework influencing the narrative model of observation perspectives as varied as feminist ethnography, contemporary psychoanalysis, hermeneutics and social constructivism. Post-structural and post-modern discourses are also potentially highly influential. Whilst these perspectives have important differences, they all recognise and work with the subjectivity inherent in the process of knowing. Psychoanalysis and ethnography have explored specifically the relationship between their knowledge base and how this shapes their view of observation. Hermeneutics, social construction theory and post-structural and post-modern discourses have influenced indirectly the narrative model via their debates about the representation of 'reality' and how we understand and construct meaning. I will consider briefly these varied contributions and move on to identify the key characteristics of the narrative model of observation.

Observation has a long association with psychoanalysis and ethnography. In both instances observation is used as a method of study and a source of understanding. Observation was valued by Freud as part of the 'science' of psychoanalysis and its contribution within the analytic world continued as psychoanalysis became influenced by ideas from phenomenology and critical theory. Observational study was introduced by Esther Bick as part of the training of child psychotherapists in 1948. There is a very close relationship between the theory and clinical methodology of psychoanalysis and psychoanalytic observation. Rustin (1989) describes psychoanalytic observation as 'an intimate, one to one personal contact whose transactions are subjected to self-reflective thought of as meticulous nature as possible' (p.54). Observation is informed, essentially, by a theory of emotionality (Briggs 1993) and, therefore, becomes more than a focused visual activity. Whilst this emotionality eschews notions of objectivity, particularly according to Rustin's ideas about standardisation and controlled conditions, the requirements of methodological rigour and responsible application are valued.

The ethnographic discourse has similarly shaped the view and use of observation. In this discourse some ethnographers aim to develop a narrative based on the insider's view, but from an objective perspective. As participant observers, they strive to achieve a rational, objective ethnography. However, the discourse is also shaped by a perspective which challenges the view that ethnography can, or should, 'occupy an uncontaminated realm of knowledge' (Whitehead 1993) – a perspective which has been developed particularly by feminist ethnographers. In this context, observation is recognised as an intersubjective process and the aim is to work with the subjectivity rather than chase the ideals of positivist science. A key debate in this discourse has focused on the observer boundary and the different perspectives on the observer's degree of involvement with the people being observed. Subjectivity does not imply uncritical absorption of information and, like psychoanalysis, emphasis is placed on the need for a space for reflection in order to understand and give meaning to the observed material.

A linked debate is concerned with the relationship between the observed, the observer and the production of knowledge. For feminist ethnographers, relinquishing the role of the 'objective expert' allows a greater opportunity for the voice of the observed to shape the narrative. It also facilitates a movement away from dichotomous opposites to the possibility of a multiplicity of meanings being given to the observation. This debate hinges on the recognition of power relations and that ethnography, the production of narratives and, hence, observation exist within the context of power – a point to which I will return.

The concern of psychoanalysis and ethnography with the representation of reality and the relationship between the observer and the observed can be located within broader debates within the social sciences, and, more generally, within late-twentieth century socio-political discourse. For example, social construction theory (Berger and Luckmann 1967) has challenged the narrative assumption that reality exists in a pure form and is waiting simply to be discovered by the independent enquirer. Reality, it is argued, is shaded differently for each individual. This diversity in the interpretation of reality is managed through the discourse of language. Reality becomes a shared social construct through the use of language which objectifies and reduces meaning. Language, essentially, objectifies experience and, in so doing, enables it to be shared. The concept of hierarchies is relevant here in terms of recognising whose definition of reality predominates.

Language and its role in the representation of reality represents another important strand of debate. Hermeneutic philosophers argue that 'there is no way in which human beings can apprehend the "true nature" of reality, all learning is mediated through language and the theories embedded in that language' (Henkel 1995, p.71). The hermeneutic tradition, therefore, contributes ideas about the relative and subjective nature of language and meaning. A multiplicity of meanings may be located within a recording and cannot be considered outside of the relationship between the text and the individual. Embedded within the philosophy are ideas about action. Consensus and the elimination of distortion in meaning require openness and free communication. Consensus also involves the sharing of ideas and, potentially, a commitment to shifting positions.

Post-structuralism and post-modernism, although different from each other, are extensions of hermeneutic philosophy and are influential trends in contemporary thinking about representation and the construction of meaning. In this way of thinking, the attempt to develop universal categories of experience, representation and explanation are 'illusory' (Parton 1994). This rejection of teleological and essentialist explanations introduces important ideas about context, complexity and conflict in the representation of reality and the development of meaning. From this perspective, truth and reality are located within a specific culture, time and place; thinking cannot be isolated from its context. Given this specificity, there will be a range of contexts, all of which exist in different relationships to power. The outcome is fragmented and conflictual versions of reality will change in relation to time, geography and ideology.

How do these varied perspectives inform the narrative model of observation within social work education and practice? It is important to stress that I am not implying an essential similarity between these perspectives. There are significant differences between some of them, for example post-modernism and psychoanalysis, whereas others, such as hermeneutics and post-modernism, share more overlapping boundaries. However, their thinking, debates and the mutual challenge to positivism have informed and shaped the narrative model. In trying to define the narrative model of observation, I would suggest it possesses the following characteristics.

The model considers reality to be primarily a personal construct. The observer is not an objective expert elucidating an essential truth but is located within the theatre of the observed and subject to the same human frailties. In this context, the observation will be determined by what a particular observer sees, and what is seen, registered and thought about will be influenced by the personal and social context of the observation. The model recognises that truth and reality are mediated through, and constructed by, the observer. By implication, the model accepts that other observers may determine a different reality and, similarly, the observational text is likely to hold a multiplicity of meanings for the reader. The observer therefore needs to engage in a debate about the resulting material – a debate in which consensus cannot be guaranteed, rather difference, conflict and uncertainty will need to be tolerated and worked with.

In this model observation is more than a visual activity. Instead, it is a complex, layered process involving looking and emotional engagement. It is also a reflective process which shapes the observation and the material generated by it. Observers do not seek to eliminate obstacles to objective reality but try to understand and make use of the thoughts and feelings generated by the experience as they are important sources of information.

An holistic approach is a significant characteristic of the model, holistic in that the observer does not attempt to dislocate slices of behaviour from their context. However, whilst attempting to develop a coherent narrative which reflects the multiple dimensions of the observed person's experience, the model works within the constraints imposed by the limits of the observer's knowledge. It also tolerates ambiguity and tries to avoid the rigid application of theory in order to make sense of material.

The observer also needs to pay attention to the construction of the observation into a written report. The model recognises that both what the text recalls and the language chosen to code behaviour and experience together represent only one potential lens for understanding the material. It is the final stage in the personal reconstruction of the observation and the meaning ascribed to it. Decisions about the transcription of the text experienced by the observer – for example, level of detail, what is omitted, the vocabulary used – are relevant to the discussion and process of understanding the material. I have focused here on the written text as this remains the most common form of recording observations, although I recognise that some of the same dilemmas occur when using either video or audio recordings. Advances in technology do not obviate the difficulties.

Observation and Current Social Work Practice

I believe that the differences between the epistemological traditions of observation identified here are central to an understanding of not only the paradoxes I have discussed but also of current ideas about observation which are evident in both social work practice and education. It is important to recognise the location of observation in relation to the two models I have described, not only to avoid normative assumptions but also because the way in which observation is characterised affects its purpose and use. I will explore this argument by discussing two prevailing debates within social work: the development of ideas about competency and reflective practice in social work. These debates illustrate significant differences in the nature of observation.

Observation and the Competency Debate

Currently, the framework of social work education is dominated by ideas about competence to practice defined as 'the ability to perform the activities within an occupation or function to the standards expected in employment. Competence is a wide concept which embodies the ability to transfer skills and knowledge to new situations within the occupational area...' (Training Agency, quoted in Burke 1989, p.1). There is widespread agreement that direct observation is a fundamental method of collecting evidence in assessment (CCETSW 1991, 1995; Kemshall 1993; O'Hagan 1996). Although written evidence can be significant, Eraut (1994) argues that 'For many types of competence...direct observation is the most valid and sometimes the only acceptable method of collecting evidence' (p.201).

The origins and characteristics of ideas about competence are embedded in what I have described as the scientific model of knowledge. Eraut (1994) traces the origins of these ideas to struggles about inclusion and exclusion within the professions – specifically, who was sufficiently 'competent' to practice law. He goes on to argue that the earliest examples of competency-based training were developed in America after the Second World War. Following the positivist tradition at this time, they 'relied heavily on task analysis based on structured observation to derive their specifications of competency and were often oblivious to the normative judgements made during the process' (p.169). Currently, ideas about the use of a competency-based approach have developed in a political context in which the significance of the market, competition and value for money are all important characteristics. Hodkinson and Issitt (1995) summarize the characteristics of the prevailing ideology: '...this thinking rejected the "nanny state", suggesting that the country needed to free up individual responsibility and choice. During this period, industrial and manufacturing metaphors for educational and social provision proliferated. All this thinking gave rise to a new ideal-type of provision, that of the market or "quasi-market"' (p.3). Reflecting some of these themes, competence in social work is characterised by an emphasis on performance and outcomes, as well as the measurement of ability and observation of tasks (Jones and Joss 1995; Shardlow and Doel 1996).

A key aspect of competency-based approaches in the public sector is to establish consistency in the quality of service delivery. Jessup (1990) explains this shift towards competency as a means of establishing more details and specific standards, in contrast to the more 'generalised and loose concept of standards which has prevailed...in the past' (p.1). It was envisaged that this approach would also improve the quality and quantity of training, particularly in relation to those groups of staff whose training needs had frequently been neglected. To this end, it was hoped that competency would have a clear role in protecting the public from incompetency (Shardlow and Doel 1996). In his defence of the use of the competence framework in social work education and practice, O'Hagan (1996) argues that since the revision of Paper 30, it is now possible to identify less reductionist approaches to competency, which now incorporate additional elements including knowledge, skills and values. O'Hagan further argues that the consistent critiques of competence fail to take account of these changes and are frequently initiated by those who have not been trained within a competency framework and do not, therefore, 'own' this approach. It is important to recognise that the competency framework is the subject of continuing debate within social work education. However, within the range of developments taking place, observation remains a central tool of the measurement of competence, particularly in relation to assessment. This tool is currently characterised by the visual focus on the observation of objective behaviour in the real world.

Observation and Reflective Practice

The competency approach and the scientific concept of observation has been challenged by academics and practitioners who are concerned with the lack of attention given to the cognitive and emotional processes attendant on the social work task. In part, this response can be considered as the emergence of a counter-culture embracing an epistemology and politics which directly contradict the principles of the prevailing competency model. This model is characterised by an interest in process as well as outcomes, an emphasis on the value of the reflexive nature of knowledge and action and an emphasis on the role of critical reflection within practice. It is also argued that social work is more than a technical activity requiring the application of a repertoire of knowledge, skills and theory. Such technocratic deconstruction of the role does not equip workers to practice in an environment which is fragmentary, complex and rapidly changing (Gould and Taylor 1996; Jennings and Kennedy 1996; Jones and Joss 1995).

While I have located ideas about competence within the positivist, scientific paradigm, I believe that another major debate in social work – the development of reflective practice – is firmly located within the development of the narrative tradition. The intellectual and emotional processes involved in reflective practice are complex and have been considered at length elsewhere (Gould and Taylor 1996; Hull and Redfern 1996; Jennings and Kennedy 1996). Reflective practice involves the practitioner in a continuous internal dialogue in which the relationship between the professional self and the personal self is kept alive and thought about (see Chapter Four). The capacity to engage in this dialogue can help practitioners to understand and develop their practice and knowledge. 'It is this potential to extend professional knowledge which makes the process of reflection much more than just thinking about practice' (Hull and Redfern 1996, p.93).

Many others within this book and elsewhere have identified the relationship between a narrative model of observation and reflection (Briggs 1995; Le Riche and Tanner 1996; Trowell and Miles 1991). Infant and child observation programmes within the narrative tradition have been recognised as making an important contribution to reflective learning and practice. In essence, it seems that the unique experience of the observer role, the recording of the observation and the opportunity to digest and explore the material in a seminar setting facilitates the multi-layered dialogue identified above. The exploration of the observer's personal experience, together with the formal content of the observation and the professional and theoretical knowledge base of the seminar group, enables a cognitive and emotional integration of personal professional practice to occur.

Observation within the competency and reflective practitioner frameworks share the common aim of contributing to the development of responsible, knowledgeable practitioners. However, the conceptualisation, method of implementation and use of observation is entirely different and is the product of the epistemological differences informing these frameworks of practice.

A potential, but yet underdeveloped, characteristic of both models is the recognition that observation is the product of power relationships. Issues of power relations pervade observation. Yet, to date,the models within social work education and practice have not developed any consistent analysis of how this relationship is manifested and managed. This is a task which will be attempted in the following chapter.

References

Berger, P.L. and Luckmann, T. (1967) *The Social Construction of Reality.* London: Allen Lane.

Briggs, S. (1993) *The Science of Observation.* Tavistock Clinic Paper No. 157 (Unpublished).

Briggs, S. (1995) 'From subjectivity to realism: child observation and social work.' In M. Yelloly and M. Henkel (eds) *Learning and Teaching in Social Work. Towards Reflective Practice.* London: Jessica Kingsley Publishers.

Burke, J.W. (ed) (1989) *Competency-Based Education and Training.* Lewes: Falmer Press.

CCETSW (1989, 1991, 1995) *Rules and Requirements for the Diploma in Social Work.* London: CCETSW.

Dean, R.G. (1989) 'Ways of knowing in clinical practice.' *Clinical Social work Journal 17,* 2, 116–127.

Dearden, G. (1979) 'Student learning and teacher instruction in an undergraduate engineering laboratory.' Unpublished PhD thesis. Institute of Educational Technology, University of Surrey.

Eraut, M. (1994) *Developing Professional Knowledge and Competence.* London: Falmer Press.

Evertson, C.M. and Green, J.L. (1986) 'Observation as inquiry and method.' In M.C. Wittrock (ed) *Handbook of Research on Teaching* (3rd Edition). New York: Macmillan.

Fairhurst, E. (1990) 'Doing ethnography in a geriatric unit.' In S. Peace (ed) *Researching Social Gerontology. Concepts, Methods and Issues.* London: Sage.

Fawcett, M. (1996) *Learning Through Child Observation.* London: Jessica Kingsley Publishers.

Featherstone, B. and Fawcett, B. (1995) 'Oh no! Not more isms: feminism, postmodernism, poststructuralism and social work education.' *Social Work Education 14,* 3, 25–43.

Flanders, N. (1984) 'Analysing teaching behaviour.' In M. Pope and J. Gilbert (eds) *Doing Research into Teaching and Learning. Module L. Diploma in the Practice of Higher Education.* Institute of Educational Development: University of Surrey.

Fry, M. (1966) *Old Age Looks at Itself.* London: The National Old People's Welfare Council.

Gould, N. and Taylor, I. (1996) 'Introduction: social work education and the "crisis of the professions".' In N. Gould and I. Taylor (eds) *Reflective Learning for Social Work*. Aldershot: Arena.

Hammersley, M. and Atkinson, P. (1983) *Ethnography. Principles and Practice*. London: Tavistock.

Henkel, M. (1995) 'Conceptions of knowledge and social work education.' In M. Yelloly and M. Henkel (eds) *Learning and Teaching in Social Work. Towards Reflective Practice*. London: Jessica Kingsley Publishers.

Hodkinson, P. and Issitt, M. (eds) (1995) *The Challenge of Competence*. London: Cassell.

Hughes, J. (1980) *The Philosophy of Social Research*. London: Longman.

Hull, C. and Redfern, L. (1996) *Profiles and Portfolios*. Basingstoke: Macmillan.

Jennings, C. and Kennedy, E. (eds) (1996) *The Reflective Professional in Education. Psychological Perspectives in Changing Contexts*. London: Jessica Kingsley Publishers.

Jessup, G. (1990) 'National Vocational Qualifications: implications for further education.' In M. Bees and M. Swords (eds) (1996) *National Vocational Qualifications and Further Education*. London: Kogan Page.

Jones, S. and Joss, R. (1995) 'Models of professionalism.' In M. Yelloly and M. Henkel (eds) *Learning and Teaching in Social Work. Towards Reflective Practice*. London: Jessica Kingsley Publishers.

Kemshall, H. (1993) 'Assessing competence: scientific process or subjective inference? Do we really see it?' *Social Work Education 12*, 1, 36–45.

Le Grand, J. and Bartlett, W. (eds) (1993) *Quasi-markets and Social Policy*. Basingstoke: Macmillan.

Le Riche, P. and Tanner, K. (1996) 'The way forward: developing an equality model of observation for social work education and practice.' *Issues in Social Work Education*.

O'Hagan, K. (ed) (1996) *Competence in Social Work Practice. A Guide for Professionals*. London: Jessica Kingsley Publishers.

Parlett, M. (1984) 'Notes on observation: unpublished handout.' In M. Pope and J. Gilbert (eds) *Doing Research into Teaching and Learning. Module L. Diploma in the Practice of Higher Education*. Institute of Educational Development: University of Surrey.

Parton, N. (1994) '"Problematics of Government": (Post) Modernity and social work.' *British Journal of Social Work 24*, 9–32.

Peberdy, A. (1993) 'Observing.' In P. Shakespeare, D. Atkinson and S. French (eds) *Reflecting in Research Practice. Issues in Health and Social Welfare*. Buckingham: Open University Press.

Pope, M. and Gilbert, J. (eds) (1984) *Doing Research into Teaching and Learning. Module L. Diploma in the Practice of Higher Education*. Institute of Educational Development: University of Surrey.

Reissman, C.K. (1993) 'Teaching research: beyond the storybook image of positivist science.' *Journal of Teaching in Social Work 8*, 1–2, 281–303.

Rossiter, A. (1996) 'Finding meaning for social work in transitional times: reflections on change.' In N. Gould and I. Taylor (eds) *Reflective Learning for Social Work*. Aldershot: Arena.

Rustin, M. (1991) *The Good Society and the Inner World Psychoanalysis, Politics and Culture.* London: Verso.

Rustin, M. (1989) 'Observing infants: reflections on methods.' In L. Miller, M. Rustin, M. Rustin and J. Shuttleworth (eds) *Closely Observed Infants.* London: Duckworth Press.

Shardlow, S. and Doel, M. (1996) *Practice Learning and Teaching.* London: Macmillan Press.

Sommer, R. and Sommer, B. (1980) *A Practical Guide to Behavioural Research.* New York: Oxford University Press.

Trowell, J. and Miles, G. (1991) 'The contribution of observation training to professional development in social work.' *Journal of Social Work Practice 5*, 1, 51–60.

Weade, G. and Evertson, C.M. (1991) 'On what can be learned by observing teaching.' *Theory into Practice XXX*, 1, 37–45.

Whitehead, J. (1993) 'From field to faculty club: framing the face of universal hu(man)ity.' *Resources for feminist research 22*, 3–4, 19–22.

Wilson, K. (1992) 'The place of child observation in social work training.' *Journal of Social Work Practice 6*, 1, 37–47.

CHAPTER TWO

Towards an Equality Model
Observation Through a Power Lens

Karen Tanner

Introduction

The last chapter argued that observation has been a significant concept in social work whether it was located within the scientific model influenced by positivist ideas about accurate recording, understanding and evaluation of the 'real' world or in the narrative model with its emphasis on the use of subjectivity, the search for meaning(s) and acceptance of diversity and complexity. It also charted the development of the concept from its central function as a tool of assessment in social work education through to the use of observational techniques in assessment and direct work with clients, particularly children and families.

In this chapter I will continue to develop these arguments by describing a third model of observation, which, in earlier articles, has been called the Equality Model (Le Riche and Tanner 1996). Quoting Abramovitz, Phillipson (1992) has used the metaphor of a lens to look at how an awareness of gender issues can inform social work practice and education. In her view, the application of a gender lens offers a means of counteracting the partiality of writing in the social sciences in favour of men. In extending this metaphor, I will introduce the concept of the power lens to models of observation since it has been argued that this perspective has frequently been lacking in relation to its use in social work (Kearney and Le Riche 1993). The application of a power lens enables any area under discussion, in this case observation, to focus on and clarify the significance of issues of inequality and disadvantage. Such a perspective also aims to work towards change. In developing a model of observation which highlights these issues, I will then move on to identify some of its characteristics as they are grounded in practice.

Before discussing these issues in greater detail, I want to develop further the idea of congruence which has already been introduced in relation to competence and reflective practice. Observation has proved to be a flexible concept which has responded to developments in a range of epistemologies. These developments need to continue for observation to respond both to changing theoretical approaches and the political and social context within which social work is located. The first part of this chapter will, therefore, discuss observation in relation to some current debates in theory development, social work values and the legislative framework.

Observation and Theory Development

> Reflexivity emphasises that the interpretation of the social world is no straightforward matter. It is not simply a matter of a sufficiently attentive gaze of the observer upon unproblematic reality (Sheppard 1995, p.175).

This statement emphasises the contentious and uncertain nature of theory in current discussions, but, as Sheppard has pointed out, this uncertainty is not a new phenomenon. The location of social work theory within the social sciences has traditionally been problematic and theoretical developments have lacked consensus both in terms of the overall characteristics of 'social work' as a phenomenon and its political and ideological roots. Additionally, there have always been questions from practitioners about the relevance of any of this argument to the work taking place in practice (Marsh and Triseliotis 1997). These debates continue to be sharpened by a political context which has challenged the expertise of professionals in an attempt to strengthen the position of the consumer (Hodkinson and Issitt 1995; Jones and Joss 1995). In relation to developments in community care and case management, Sheppard discusses the role of the social worker as state functionary. He argues that the nature of social work has always been 'significantly determined by the function of the agency in which the social worker is practising'. This is particularly true of state social work which '...is about particular roles carried out in pursuit of agency function and designated by law' (p.42). The climate of 'new managerialism' which pervades the development of community care in England has, therefore, brought about further changes in the nature of the social work role. This has traditionally involved tasks and functions which include both discretionary and rule-based elements. In Sheppard's view, the balance has now been tipped in favour of an emphasis on following rules.

A further example of some of the characteristics of this 'new managerialism' within social work is provided by Everitt and Hardiker's (1996) analysis of different models of evaluation. They identify the prevailing rational/technical model of evaluating effectiveness as having similar characteristics and priorities to those already ascribed to 'new managerialism'. 'Evaluation is...rapidly becoming part of the repertoire of those controlling policy and resource allocation measures' (p.83). They describe other characteristics of this model, including its failure to recognise the significance of power and status in influencing the process and outcomes of evaluation, a top-down approach and a desire for consensus. This last point suggests that relatively little attention is paid to diversity of opinion and this approach provides few opportunities for debate, particularly around conflicting morality or values.

Within social work knowledge there has always been a strand of theory building which has argued for the development of ideas about social work as a counter-culture, taking up a position of challenge in opposition to prevailing orthodoxies. This point of view remains significant in spite of (or because of) the prevalence of mainstream ideas such as those already described. For example, Everitt and Hardiker (1996) suggest that alternative approaches to evaluation could be developed which reflect some of the characteristics of critical social science. Such a model would be committed to change and would challenge the commonly accepted ways of viewing 'success' and 'effectiveness'. It would also adopt a perspective which locates individuals within their context – for example analysing why some voices are heard in the evaluation process and others are not. Perhaps most relevant to the arguments presented here, this approach would be committed to equality and change and would also recognise the political processes which surround assessments of 'good practice'. Since such judgements contain strong elements of subjectivity, such a model would have to have an 'understanding of the relationship between subjectivity and power' (p.102). This last point suggests that evaluation is not only a product of prevailing ways of thinking but should also attempt to challenge and change such processes.

Sheppard (1995) suggests that case management has to adopt a similarly critical and reflexive approach if it is to retain a social work perspective in response to the view that professional knowledge and skills are not necessary qualifications for the task. Sheppard's discussion of the concept of reflexivity is relevant to the development of the Equality Model of observation. He argues that reflexivity is significant in qualitative sociology and defines it as 'a form of self-reflection; of other reflection; and a processual way of making sense of social circumstances and social life' (p.173). Reflexivity contains three elements: self-reflection, including reflection on our thoughts as well as our actions, the search for explanations of our actions and monitoring the actions of ourselves and others. This process is not dissimilar to Everitt and Hardiker's (1996) description of the two distinct layers of evaluation, producing the evidence and then making judgements. Murrell (1993) also describes two phases of observational judgement: the process stage and the inference stage. In the process stage a large amount of data is collected before any judgements are made about the material. The inference stage is when this material is ordered and evaluated. All these authors argue for the need to reflect on material before making judgements. By emphasising process and giving it equal importance to content and outcome, Sheppard recognises the significance of retaining a critical response to both theoretical and practice debates.

Reflexivity also emphasises differences of perspective and opinion and the necessity of valuing this diversity. This view is particularly significant in relation to the position of clients within the reflexive process and the need to take account of the views of clients, service users, consumers or customers. These titles highlight the differing ideological perspectives underlying the increased pressure to involve clients in the decision-making processes of which they are a central part. This reflects a major preoccupation in social work which is proving easier to espouse than it is to put into practice, particularly in the current context of welfare and state social work (Wise 1985). None the less, in the context of anti-discriminatory and anti-oppressive practice this is an issue which has to be central to good practice in observation and its implications will be discussed further. It is apparent that in the current climate there are few absolutes in theory or in practice, a situation which also applies to the values that underpin social work.

Observation and Values

The development of the Equality Model of observation is influenced by a number of concerns, one of the most significant of which is that the model should be congruent with the value-base of social work. Current writing about morality and values within social work has demonstrated a high level of agreement both about the content of the debate and its implications for theory and practice (Hugman and Smith 1995; Shardlow 1989). Statements about values have moved from the universal, overarching categorisations which Hugman and Smith describe as 'classical', to a perspective which argues that value statements are 'highly contentious'. Ethics and values are political phenomena and are, therefore, open to dispute from different perspectives both inside and outside the profession (Hugman and Smith 1995). Biestek's (1961) seven categories and Butrym's (1976) three principles both sought to identify broad statements which would be relevant to all social works agencies and circumstances. These principles included unconditional respect for individuals, client self-determination and a belief in the uniqueness of each individual. As these principles showed, values were developed from a perspective which was primarily concerned about the way in which an individual social worker related to an individual client. There was little, if any, acknowledgement of social work as a socially defined process influenced by the legal, organisational and social context within which it took place (Hugman and Smith 1995). Although the nature of social work continues to retain this individualised perspective, value statements have to take account of the effects of change, conflict and complexity (Shardlow 1989).

The impact of these views on the discussion of values has been to recognise that the attempt to formulate a set of universal values applicable to every situation is fruitless. This is partly because of the recognition of the complexity referred to above but also due to the lack of consensus about the 'right' course of action in individual circumstances. Social work has never been based on a consensus about goals and the recognition of different perspectives has now led to an approach which argues for the development of values which are 'grounded in everyday concerns' rather than the product of universal categories (Hugman and Smith 1995). Current debates are attempting to develop an understanding of more general dilemmas from the specifics of practice rather than the other way round (Cheetham 1989; Sheppard 1995; Wise 1995). The effect of this case-by-case approach has been to highlight issues such as the division between personal and professional roles and values, the range of choices available in terms of action and the impact of power and difference in relationships. In this context, Cheetham (1989) suggests that social workers should seek to 'avoid instant judgements and moral absolutes...' (p.41) while Wise (1995) looks to feminist ethics to provide a framework within which to practice state social work. This case-by-case approach continues to recognise the centrality of values and ethics within social work practice but seeks a more concrete response to current dilemmas.

One of the central dilemmas with which a discussion of values needs to be concerned is how to incorporate a power perspective into practice. The radical social work tradition sought to do this by regarding social work as the product of political processes. This inevitably meant that the position of those receiving social work help was located within the context of poverty and disadvantage. Thus individual problems were the product of social processes and social workers were in a powerful position both in terms of exercising control and providing resources. Hugman and Smith (1995) argue that this perspective has recently been influential in the development of professional codes of ethics and the requirements for the DipSW qualification in social work: 'Although still founded on primarily liberal principles involving the recognition of competing value positions, social workers are now expected to develop an awareness of structural oppression, understand and counteract stigma and discrimination of both individual and institutional kinds, and promote policies and practices which are non-discriminatory and anti-oppressive' (p.7). Although non-discrimination and anti-oppression are included in these requirements and an anti-oppressive perspective was initially prominent, these issues remain contentious and have been modified in subsequent revisions. As Hugman and Smith argue, 'contention is inbuilt', but discussions on ethics now reflect an awareness of the centrality of power relations in practice, even if there are disagreements about responses in the current political climate.

In common with the theoretical approaches already outlined, value debates emphasise the need for practitioners to be both reflective and reflexive in responding to the dilemmas and choices which face them. Hugman and Smith (1995) quote Husband's ideas about the need for 'morally active' practitioners who are self-critical and concerned to reflect on the motives behind their actions. They also need to be aware of the impact of their own race, class and gender – for example in determining their approach to assessment, planning and all aspects of practice. This is particularly necessary in a profession where value decisions are central and where ethics are related to action – 'ethically informed practice is essential if the rights and welfare of service users/clients are to be protected' (Hugman and Smith 1995, p.12).

Legislation, Partnership and Observation

The third debate I wish to raise is how ideas about empowerment and partnership, embodied in current legislation, also influence the equality model of observation in social work.

Social work is mainly organised within a legislative framework that informs and regulates practice. The implementation of the 1989 Children Act in England followed by the Children (Scotland) Act 1995 and the 1990 National Health Service and Community Care Act introduced a new statutory framework for working with children and their families and adults in need of care. Both pieces of legislation are imbued with a philosophy which has been fundamentally important in determining their content and subsequent implementation – by this I mean the 1989 Children Act's emphasis on partnership with parents and the cornerstone position of client empowerment within the National Health Service and Community Care Act: '…the ideal of empowerment stemming from the National Health Service and Community Care Act and partnership with parents from the Children Act, are based upon a similar philosophy and require similar working practices' (Stevenson and Parsloe 1993, p.8). This philosophy is complex and chameleon-like (Turney 1997, in a personal communication to the author) as, in part, it reflects the conservative preoccupation with marketisation, the enterprise culture and consumer choice, but it also appeals to liberal and radical concerns with issues of inequality and the misuse of power. I want to explore the implications of these ideas as I believe they lend themselves to developing a congruent model of observation in social work.

Examination of the two pieces of primary legislation reveals that they rarely specifically address partnership or empowerment. The spirit of the legislation and the meaning of the concepts has emerged from the supporting guidance and government-sponsored training materials and literature – for example the Family Rights Group and the National Institute for Social Work publications.

The government guidance *Care Management and Assessment: Practitioners' Guide* (DoH/SSI and Scottish Office 1991) states:

> the rationale for this reorganisation (of care services) is the empowerment of users and carers. Instead of users and carers being subordinate to the wishes of service providers, the roles will be progressively adjusted. In this way, users and carers will be enabled to exercise the same power as consumers of other services. This redressing of the bal-

ance of power is the best guarantee of a continuing improvement in the quality of service. (p.9)

It further identifies the core values underpinning the delivery of services which should be reflected in the policies and practices of agencies, namely:

- rights of citizenship
- respect for independence
- regard for privacy
- recognition of dignity and individuality
- individual choice
- promotion of an individual's aspirations and abilities.

Working Together: A Guide to Arrangements for Inter-Agency Co-operation for the Protection of Children from Abuse identifies the need to work in partnership with families; 'as parental responsibility for children is retained notwithstanding any court orders short of adoption, local authorities must work in partnership with parents' (DoH 1991, p.1). An influential definition of partnership was subsequently provided by the Family Rights Group (1991) in their publication *The Children Act 1989: Working in Partnership with Families*. They identify the following as characteristics of partnership:

- respect for one another
- rights to information
- accountability
- competence and value accorded to any individual's contribution.

This definition is expanded further by *The Challenge of Partnership in Child Protection: Practice Guide* (DoH/SSI 1995) which introduces 'fifteen essential principles for working in partnership', which include the following themes:

- respect and confidentiality
- openness
- a focus on the child but recognising the wider familial, cultural and social context
- the use of supervision to reflect on the process of the work
- a balanced approach which recognises strengths and weaknesses.

Implicit within all this guidance is a recognition that empowerment and partnership and their constituent principles are both goals and processes (Stevenson and Parsloe 1993). Partnership may be a desired goal in working with a family but can only be achieved by engaging in a process in which the beliefs and principles are put into practice: 'It is this marriage of philosophy and practice that may succeed in turning good intention into reality' (Jackson, Fisher and Ward 1996, p.13).

The sentiments at the heart of these principles are to be welcomed but they are ideals which, once they are applied, become more complex and ambiguous. Reconciling the different needs and rights of children, parents, users and carers may be difficult and the implementation of partnership and empowerment will not be straightforward. Similarly, at the beginning of a working relationship between practitioner and client, co-operation, trust and certainty may not be at a premium. The attempt to work together may be fraught and conflictual and ideas of partnership resisted. The process may also be subject to fluctuation as the relationship is affected by new events, stresses and external pressures.

The psychological and emotional dimensions of the process also need to be acknowledged. The involvement of social workers may frequently be perceived by individuals and families as interfering and indicating a loss of control and diminished personal effectiveness and autonomy. Paradoxically in these circumstances, empowerment may be experienced as a reinforcement of diminished personal power. Similarly, practitioners may also be fearful of the professional losses heralded by empowerment – for example control of the process and sharing information. Despite the evidence of research (Thoburn, Lewis and Shemmings 1995) which suggests that practice based on the principles of partnership is more likely to achieve successful outcomes, empowerment can be perceived as a threat to practitioners. Empowerment, therefore, is an ongoing and evolving process which will require constant re-evaluation and, if necessary, re-negotiation.

The process of empowerment and partnership extends beyond the individual relationship between the practitioner and client to the organisation, where again paradoxes and complexities exist. Many practitioners, whilst committed to the idea of empowerment, may themselves feel disempowered due to inadequate departmental resources and concerns about the capacity of the independent sector to deliver services (Stevenson and Parsloe 1993). Similarly, mechanistic bureaucracy and decline in professional autonomy can impact significantly on a practitioner's creativity and enthusiasm for empowerment and partnership. The ensuing paradox is that of the 'disempowered empowerer'. As Stevenson and Parsloe argue, 'empowerment is about processes which permeate organisations and professional thought. The challenge is to create a culture in which such processes are able to thrive' (p.59). Despite all these difficulties, I consider that empowerment and partnership are worth striving for, otherwise there is a danger of them becoming ritualistic rhetoric.

Bridging the Gap Towards an Equality Model of Observation

I have been trying to argue that critical areas of social work have included debates about power, user involvement and context. Models and approaches to observation need to engage in the same debates, both in relation to the process of observation and its contribution to anti-oppressive learning and practice. Baldwin (1994) is one of the few writers about observation who has specifically drawn attention to these issues.

In Baldwin's article discussing the role of observation in work with children and families it is possible to identify a number of themes relevant to this debate. The central argument is that observational skills are core skills for anti-oppressive practice and that existing models have not sufficiently emphasised this aspect of observation. Baldwin begins by discussing observation in its historical context, arguing that theoretical models of child development have been produced by research which has been largely male, white and eurocentric. Theoretical approaches have also been individualistic. Baldwin discusses the dilemmas involved in valuing the unique experience of the individual child within the overall picture of 'normal behaviour': 'One of the principle issues emerging from the child development literature and reflected in the social work educational material concerns the tension between the observed child as a unique individual on the one hand, and as a child demonstrating an example of normative behaviour, on the other hand' (1994, p.76). In the process of placing individuals in their context, observers need to 'get beyond the individual and understand the collective experience' (p.81).

In spite of having what Baldwin describes as a 'large feelings agenda', the observation of children and families in social work has tended to pay exclusive attention to the feelings of the observer. The balance of this agenda needs to change, since recognition of the voice of the observed in the observation process is critical for Baldwin: 'Hearing and valuing the voice of the observed is a fundamental principle' (p.83). He makes connection between the 'invisibility' of the person being observed and issues of power and powerlessness. In child abuse inquiries, the voice of children has not been heard because they are not a valued group in society. The same could be said to be true of other disadvantaged groups, such as black people, older people and people with disabilities. Unless these issues related to the dynamics of power are acknowledged, the process of observation can be experienced as oppressive.

In terms of the outcomes of observation, Baldwin identifies a number of observational skills which are transferable to social work practice as a whole. These include maintaining openness and concentration, being able to use theoretical material and being aware of our own prejudices. For Baldwin, the role of observation in contributing to anti-oppressive practice enables the observer to take account of and reflect on 'stereotypical pictures, prejudicial views and oppressive beliefs' (p.79).

Baldwin's ideas are helpful in shaping an Equality Model of observation since they recognise 'the relationship between individuals and their environment' (p.82). This environment is characterised by inequality and oppression, where all relationships are affected by a power dynamic. Social work has always emphasised the significance of individual experience; it has developed to take account of social processes and to make connections between the individual and those processes. In parallel with these developments, observation needs to have an awareness of the significance of power permeating the model in all aspects. These include the relationship between the observer and observed, power relations within the observational system and the power the observer has in creating the written material. While these broad power differentials in terms of role and task are significant, we also need to be aware of the effects of other pervasive inequalities. The interlocking differences of race, class and gender, for instance, will impact on the observation process. These issues will always be factors in the dynamics of observation and need to be recognised and worked with (Kemshall 1993). This perspective on power also needs to be applied to the outcomes of observation, whether these are assessments in practice or learning in an educational setting. I would agree with Baldwin that observation makes a significant contribution to anti-oppressive practice. The application of a power lens is transformational, both in terms of the process and outcome, of observation.

In the last part of this chapter I attempt to ground the Equality Model in practice. In order to do this I have chosen three aspects of observation practice illustrating the model in action. The negotiation process demonstrates the significance of the power lens and some of the complexities involved in trying to incorporate the perspective of the observed. The recording of the written material is concerned with the construction of meaning, the uniqueness of the observation and engaging with the view of the reader.

Finally, I will to return to ideas about reflection, specifically in terms of its contribution to power relations. Together, the processes of negotiation, recording and reflection are concerned with both the process and outcomes of observation. Although the examples given in this discussion are from an Infant and Child Observation sequence on a DipSW programme, they illustrate issues relevant to observation in all other situations.

Negotiating the Observation

As identified throughout this book, observation can be used in a wide range of settings. In some contexts observation's primary function is as a tool for education and learning – for example the inclusion of observation in DipSW programmes and the training of Approved Social Workers (ASWs). Here observation is a means of developing and deepening the observer's knowledge and understanding about a particular client group, curriculum area and of themselves as individuals and practitioners.

In practice agencies observation is an important tool of enquiry and assessment. Observation may be included in a comprehensive assessment to determine the level of risk to a child within his or her family. Similarly, it is a helpful tool for consultants, managers and supervisors to understand and assess staff and agency functioning. In the practice agency observation is clearly an important source of learning but its purpose is different and there are likely to be action-based implications of the knowledge produced. The structure of observation in this context has to be carefully supervised and managed since it is a central part of the agency's primary task.

Practice teaching and practice assessing are further examples of the use of observation. CCETSW requires that DipSW students are observed on three occasions during their practice placement and trainee practice teachers are observed by a practice assessor on at least two occasions (CCETSW 1989, 1991, 1996). Here observation is mandatory and has a combined assessment and teaching function. Power differentials are sharply defined in this hierarchy of relationships.

I would suggest that careful negotiation needs to take place among all parties to an observation, in which the context, purpose and possible outcomes are clearly identified. The status of the observer, whether as a 'learner', 'professional', 'expert' or 'assessor', has to be acknowledged and, with this, the remit of the observer's authority and power clarified. Clearly, all observers are in a powerful position as they filter and construct what is seen. The power differentials are even more stark when the purpose of the observation is primarily for assessment. Recommendations from the assessment may be perceived by the person being observed as contrary to their interests and wishes.

The management of the negotiation can be assisted if the parties to the observation can draw upon previous experiences of observation and discuss the feelings and fears generated. This is particularly pertinent in practice teaching. There is now a hierarchy of observation within practice teaching in which the student observes the client, the practice teacher observes the student and the practice assessor observes the practice teacher (Tanner and Le Riche 1995). The experience of being observed can provide important insights into the negotiation process at all points in this hierarchy. The practice teacher/assessor's ability to reflect upon the experience of being observed and assessed can make an important contribution to the management of the dynamics in the negotiation and assessment of the observation. As observation becomes more prevalent within social work, observers will be able to transfer the experience in one setting to inform other situations – that is, from practice teacher observing student to manager observing a member of staff.

In the negotiation of the observation practice, agencies have to consider the issue of feedback and when and how this takes place. Feedback is a greatly underrated skill and, if addressed thoughtfully and incorporated within a working relationship between practitioner and client and practitioner and manager for example, it can contribute to personal development and change. However, it may also be helpful in the negotiation stage to identify processes of challenge and appeal.

A key objective of open and clear negotiation of the observation is obtaining the permission of those to be observed. Frequently, this is straightforward. However, there are areas of complexity which require attention.

Even in a learning environment, anxiety about the observer role can impact on the process of negotiation. Mark, a DipSW student, writes:

I want to acknowledge the apprehension and anxieties I had about engaging in this project and how this led me to avoid setting up the observation initially. Although I felt a lot of interest in carrying out observation in the home environment, I had difficulty in justifying the project to myself as a learning activity without having the authority that would come with a professional role or the security of knowing the family personally. I had concerns about my inexperience and the impact my presence could have on a family and I felt anxious that I would be perceived as being intrusive or critical of the child's progress and the parents skills. I was also anxious about the impact of the observation on myself both emotionally and as a test of my own abilities.

Mark identifies the impact of his anxiety as a reluctance to begin the process of negotiation. Anxiety can also influence the process in other ways. A particular example is underplaying aspects of the observation which the observer perceives she, or the person being observed, may find uncomfortable. This may involve the non-interactional nature of the role or, commonly, anxieties about being perceived as judgemental. Sean, a DipSW student, writes: 'the stance I adopted was immediately defensive, I was anxious to reassure mum that I would not be looking for or analysing her skill as a parent.'

This denial of ownership can result in a shallow, fudged negotiation. Specific issues about the observation – particularly those which may involve intimacy, such as toileting and bathing and in the observation of children breastfeeding – are frequently glossed over due to the observer's fear of embarrassment. Failure to address such matters can result in the observation being experienced as intrusive and oppressive and the risk of the observation breaking down can be high.

Another common problem in the negotiation stage is determining from whom consent is required. This frequently arises in the observation of children but equally can apply to the observation of adults. In my mind, when the observation is taking place in the family home, all the carers of the child should be consulted. Here legal issues of parental responsibility need to be considered. In two-parent households the negotiation process would involve, ideally, both parents. If one parent is absent from the negotiation, their view should be sought within the discussion. In a learning setting the observer may approach a childminder or nursery to observe a child. In such settings the parents' consent must be obtained. The need for parental permission is sometimes resisted by the carer *in loco parentis*. I believe this resistance should be carefully explored and worked through. Occasionally, the exploration reveals that a child has been chosen by the nursery due to concern about his or her parenting or development and the observation is identified as a means of obtaining an assessment of the child. The observer therefore needs to ensure that she is not colluding with a covert agenda and that her role is not being perverted.

Critical, in my mind, is the position of the child. Baldwin (1994) has identified the powerlessness of the child in the observation process. Whilst I recognise that informed consent from a small child is contentious, I believe this should not prevent an explanation of the observation being given to the child (and siblings) and their views taken into consideration and discussed with parents and carers. The complexity of this process, in relation to children, is described by Roxanne, a DipSW student:

> At my first meeting with the little girl I told her that I was coming to the nursery to watch and learn about children playing. I was unsure whether she understood me but I felt it was best to leave it at that until I got to know her better. As the observations progressed, she tried to interact with me but never questioned me as to why I was there. However on the last observation she directly asked me about who I was. She used the same questions as another child had asked me on a previous observation – 'Are you a mummy?' 'Are you a teacher?' When I replied no she finally asked me 'What are you?' I explained to her that I was learning about how children play. She seemed satisfied with this answer but later in the observation she commented that I was watching her again. Looking back now I feel that I did not give enough thought to how I would explain to her what I was doing. As she had not questioned my role I wrongly assumed that she was either unaware or not interested in what I was doing. Her use of the other child's questions made me realise that she probably did not have the vocabulary or the confidence to question me earlier.

Here Roxanne identifies the thought and preparation required for a meaningful discussion with a child or adult, who, for whatever reason, may have difficulty in comprehending what is being requested of them – for example a person with Alzheimers disease or learning difficulty. Careful consideration must be given to issues such as cognitive ability, language capacity, developmental stage, and the process of negotiation adapted to meet the needs of the individual. The views should also be sought of a child's parents, or carers significant in the life of a vulnerable adult, as to when and how the negotiation will take place and who it would be helpful to involve.

Finally, the negotiation of the observation needs to consider the dimension of difference and the dynamics of power in relationships involving difference. I have considered difference in relation to role and status but here I am referring to issues of gender, race, culture, sexuality and physical ability. The observer, particularly in a learning situation, may not feel powerful or confident about the request to observe. However, the observer, by virtue of being, for example, white or male or able-bodied, will be endowed with a certain level of ascribed power within society which may make it more difficult for a black person or woman or a person with a disability to question and/or say 'no' to the observation. The observer needs to recognise how this dynamic impacts upon the process of negotiating the observation and work to empower the other individual to participate fully in the discussion and exercise a real choice. The acknowledgement of difference and its impact at this stage can also open up the discussion, which, in the long-term, assists the process of observation.

Recording the Observation

It is good practice for observations to be recorded and available in a written report, in parallel with most other forms of social work practice and education. The narrative and scientific traditions of observation within social work differ in their approach to recording. Broadly, the narrative tradition embraces a naturalistic form of presenting material whereas the scientific tradition has tended to use measurement charts and symbols (Fawcett 1996). Neither approach has located its ideas about the written communication of the observation within a framework in which power is considered. Ideas about the complexity of language exist within the narrative model and, arguably, there is more opportunity for these ideas to incorporate a power lens. The potential of this model has been influential in the development of this chapter's ideas about recording within the Equality Model.

Within an Equality Model, ideas about the use of language, the organisation of the written material and the ownership and distribution of the observation report all require consideration. The observer needs to pay careful attention to the use of language. The observer cannot assume that language is transparent but rather that language is imbued with a multiplicity of meanings which may or may not be shared. Take, for example, the recent convention to transpose the word 'wicked' to mean 'good', 'cool' and 'smart'. In other instances the difference in meaning may be more subtle – for example describing someone as 'soft' has potentially pejorative or positive connotations. It is also important to recognise different traditions in language. The meaning of language can vary between ethnic and cultural groups and between generations, and frequently has gender implications. Observation conducted across racial and cultural differences, where the language spoken in the observation is not the first language of the observer, presents an important challenge. How does the observer record her understanding of dialogue which takes place? How is a balance of dialogue and non-verbal gestures achieved? With what certainty can the observer represent her understanding of the conversation taking place?

Consideration should be given to the difficulty in finding words to describe non-verbal communications and emotions, such as a baby crying or an unwell person's expression of pain. How are such communications to be measured, evaluated and recorded on a tick box sheet? Russ, a DipSW student, reflects:

> The baby's inability to express her feelings verbally coupled with my own struggle to understand what she might be feeling resulted in a strange identification with the baby as a means of involving myself in her world. ... The process of trying to determine whether my descriptions of the baby's feelings were a reflection, rather than the superimposition of my own reality on the observation, led to an increased awareness of the ways in which my assumptions, feelings and experiences shape my perceptions.

At times, the struggle to 'find the words' is an expression of the observer's capacity to tolerate distressing situations and hold on to uncertainty. Whilst this is an important seam of reflection, it can be a painful process and the observer may require support.

The discussion so far has focused specifically on language, but consideration of the organisation of language is also required. The written picture created depends as much on the way words are knitted together as the words themselves. The representation of an observation will frequently require the observer to convey complex verbal and non-verbal interactions, rhythms and patterns, uncertainty and intensity in expressions. An example may be the attempt to capture the emotional attunement of a parent–baby relationship. Therefore, thought needs to be given to the organisation of the material:

> should (you) include silence, false starts, emphasis, non-lexicals like 'uhu', discourse markers like 'y'know', or 'so', overlapping speech and other signs of listeners participation in the narrative? Should (you) give clauses separate lines, display rhythmic and poetic structures by grouping lines? Not simply technical questions, these seemingly mundane choices – what to include, how to arrange and display the text – have serious implications for how a reader will understand the narrative. (Riessman 1993, p.294)

Given the complexity of writing, the observer must be prepared to reflect upon the use of language, its meaning on a personal and structural level, why it has been selected and organised in a particular way and why some material has been omitted. The desire for positive evaluation by others can also influence the way material is recorded. I am of the view that students and practitioners who are committed to observation within an equalities framework will endeavour to grapple with the meanings language holds. Observers within this model will also be willing to explore differences in interpretation and possible conflicts of opinion with the reader. Conflicts of opinion will be of differing orders depending on whether the observation is taking place in the learning environment on an Infant and Child Observation Project or as part of an assessment in a practice agency. As discussed earlier, procedures for managing differences in opinions need to be identified in the negotiation stage.

Finally, thought needs to be given to the issue of ownership and distribution of the report. Ideas about partnership and user involvement, already discussed, encourage the sharing of information and decision making. However, the extent of open recording is variable, ranging from the tokenistic to the regular review of case records as part of the practitioner/client relationship in which the recording is an important tool of therapeutic intervention, a model pioneered by the Family Service Unit in the United Kingdom. Similar practices are likely to exist with observation material.

Within social work education there are again different practices in relation to the sharing of recorded material. In practice teaching the sharing of the practice teacher's observations with the student is recognised as an important part of the learning process. Here the material generated by the observation is used as a means of assessment but also critically contributes to the student's learning. When the observer is in the learning role it is not always appropriate for the written material to be shared as it is a source of learning, often of a very personal nature. If the learner shares the material with the person being observed, this may introduce a distortion into the learning as the observer may consciously or unconsciously edit the report for the reader.

I recognise that there are different practices which are influenced by the purpose of the observation and the status of the observer. However, whatever the purpose and role, the ownership, access and distribution of the material has to be explored, discussed and agreed at the negotiation stage of the process.

Reflection and Observation

An Equality Model of observation recognises the contribution of reflection to understanding the dynamics of difference and power operating within an observation. The concept of reflection is frequently associated with narrative approaches to observation. It is less likely to be articulated within a scientific model but this should not preclude recognition of its value.

Let us consider how ideas about reflection can be developed within an Equality Model. Reflection is an imprecise concept. However, Boud, Keogh and Walker (1985) offer a helpful description. Reflection is 'a generic term for those intellectual and affective activities in which individuals engage to explore their experiences in order to lead to new understandings and appreciation' (p.19). It is a process grounded in the experience of the individual and requires 'giving attention to noticing what is happening in themselves and in their external environment' (Boud and Knight 1996, p.27). Schön (1983, 1987) has been highly influential in recognising reflection as a process consisting of different dimensions: reflection in action – that is, attending to thoughts and emotions while engaged in a situation – and reflection on action – returning to the situation and exploring the experience. The concept of reflection, therefore, involves ideas about careful noticing, attending to feelings and critical focused thought.

These ideas about what it means to be reflective are extended by observation both qualitatively and in terms of purpose. Observation provides an opportunity to be in a situation in a qualitatively different way. Rather than being preoccupied with activity or action, the observer role creates a space for thought and reflection. The everyday priorities are reversed, enabling attention to be focused on fine detail and the feelings evoked by the process. Sometimes, these are feelings which are suppressed by having the professional 'lid' put on them – for example the pain, disgust and anger that can be generated by the working environment or an awareness of our own racist or classist responses. Such reflection is an important part of the process of recognising the impact of thoughts and feelings on the professional self in role. These ideas are explored in more detail within this volume, particularly in Chapters Four and Five.

These issues are central when exploring ideas about difference, power, anti-discriminatory practice and anti-oppressive practice. They are important in social work education and are reflected in agency policy statements. However, the complexity of these issues often remains unarticulated. I suggest that to engage meaningfully with these ideas, practitioners must be willing to explore these complexities, which, at times, will involve thinking the unthinkable. By this I mean that practitioners need to reflect, for example, upon their personal and emotional responses to difference and explore whether they are congruent or at odds with their intellectual commitment. The capacity to reflect upon internalised prejudices and their insidious and negative impact on practice is an important first step in the struggle to develop anti-discriminatory practice and anti-oppressive practice. Observation's capacity to generate this powerful and personal self-examination is illustrated by the following observer's experiences: 'my own stereotypical views as to the nature of the black family are uncovered through the experience of undertaking observation within the home of a black family.' Similarly, another observer writes: 'I realise that what I was observing did not match the internal picture of my childhood which was to do with differences in class and parenting, and so I was rejecting it as inauthentic and staged.'

A different but equally difficult area of reflection is the relationship between a worker's practice and beliefs and the agency task and ethos. The worker may need to confront the dilemma that the agency's task may pose contradictions in relation to her beliefs. Wise (1995) highlights this dilemma in her experience of implementing feminist social work in the statutory sector. She questions whether feminist social work is possible in statutory work with children and families where the needs and rights of one group have to be prioritised over the rights of others. Agency ethos may be experienced by practitioners as demoralising and disempowering. As stated earlier, the paradox of the 'disempowered empowerer' can occur and practitioners may need to reflect on whether they are mirroring this process in the practitioner/client relationship.

If observers are willing to engage with a reflective process, there is the potential for observation to be developed as a tool for recognising, thinking about and responding to power relationships. However, this process of reflection needs to be supported by the existence of supervision structures which ensure maximum use of the reflection generated. It is important to note that these structures, whether in a seminar setting or line-management supervision, will also include complex power differentials. Kemshall (1993) argues that this process requires 'supervisors to reflect upon their own knowledge base and value system, and to consider and discuss with supervisees the difference and diversity between the knowledge system each brings' (p.43).

Conclusion

In applying a power lens to observation and describing aspects of the Equality Model I have attempted to develop a number of themes which are congruent with debates in social work practice and education. The model retains a focus on the value of accessing individual experience but, equally, acknowledges the significance of wider structural processes. This interaction influences thinking about observation both at the level of processes and outcome. In this sense it is both reflective and reflexive, requiring the observer to be self-critical at all stages.

References

Baldwin, M. (1994) 'Why observe children?' *Social Work Education 13*, 2, 74–85.

Biestek, F. (1961) *The Casework Relationship.* London: George Allen and Unwin.

Boud, D., Keogh, R. and Walker, D. (eds) (1985) *Reflection: Turning Experience into Learning.* London: Kogan Page.

Boud, D. and Knight, S. (1996) 'Course design for reflective practice.' In N. Gould and I. Taylor (eds) *Reflective Learning for Social Work.* Hants and Vermont: Arena.

Butrym, Z. (1976) *The Nature of Social Work.* London: Macmillan.

CCETSW (1989, 1991) *Rules and Requirements for the Diploma in Social Work.* London: CCETSW.

CCETSW (1996) *Rules and Requirements for the Practice Teaching Award Paper 26.4.* London: CCETSW.

Cheetham, J. (1989) 'Values in action.' In S. Shardlow (ed) *The Values of Change in Social Work.* London: Routledge.

DoH (1990) *National Health Service and Community Care Act.* London: HMSO.

DoH (1991) *Working Together: A Guide to Arrangements for Inter-Agency Co-Operation for the Protection of Children from Abuse.* London: HMSO.

DoH/SSI (1995) *The Challenge of Partnership in Child Protection: Practice Guide.* London: HMSO.

DoH/SSI and Scottish Office (1991) *Care Management and Assessment: Practitioners' Guide.* London: HMSO.

Everitt, A. and Hardiker, P. (1996) *Evaluating for Good Practice.* Basingstoke: Macmillan.

Family Rights Group (1991) *The Children Act 1989: Working in Partnership with Families.* London: HMSO.

Fawcett, M. (1996) *Learning Through Child Observation.* London: Jessica Kingsley Publishers.

Hodkinson, P. and Issitt, M. (eds) (1995) *The Challenge of Competence.* London: Cassell.

Hugman, R. and Smith, D. (1995) *Ethical Issues in Social Work.* London and New York: Routledge.

Jackson, S., Fisher, M. and Ward, H. (1996) 'Key concepts in looking after children: parenting, partnership, outcomes.' In S. Jackson and S. Kilroe (eds) *Looking After Children: Good Parenting, Good Outcomes – A Reader.* London: HMSO.

Jones, S. and Joss, R. (1995) 'Models of professionalism.' In M. Yelloly and M. Henkel (eds) *Learning and Teaching in Social Work. Towards Reflective Practice.* London: Jessica Kingsley Publishers.

Kearney, P. and Le Riche, P. (1993) 'Looking at the ordinary in a new way: the applications of feminist thinking to a post qualifying social work course.' *Social Work Education 12,* 2, 19–28.

Kemshall, H. (1993) 'Assessing competence: process or subjective inference? Do we really see it?' *Social Work Education 12,* 1, 36–45.

Le Riche, P. and Tanner, K. (1996) 'The way forward: developing an equality model of observation for social work education and practice.' *Issues in Social Work Education 16,* 2, 3–14.

Marsh, P. and Triseliotis, J. (1997) *Ready to Practice? Social Workers and Probation Officers: Their Training and First Year in Work.* Aldershot: Avebury.

Murrell (1993) 'Judgement of professional competence: bags of bias.' In M. Preston-Shoot (ed) *Assessment of Competence in Social Work Law.* Bournemouth: Social Work Education, Special Publication.

Phillipson, J. (1992) *Practicing Equality Women, Men and Social Work.* London: CCETSW.

Reissman, C.K. (1993) 'Teaching research: beyond the storybook image of positivist science.' *Journal of Teaching in Social Work 8,* 1–2, 281–303.

Schön, D. (1983) *The Reflective Practitioner: How Professionals Think in Action.* New York: Basic Books.

Schön, D. (1987) *Educating the Reflective Practitioner: Towards a New Design for Teaching and Learning in the Professions.* San Francisco: Jossey Bass.

Shardlow, S. (ed) (1989) *The Values of Change in Social Work.* London: Routledge.

Sheppard, M. (1995) *Care Management and the New Social Work: A Critical Analysis.* London: Whiting and Birch.

Stevenson, O. and Parsloe, P. (1993) *Community Care and Empowerment.* York: Joseph Rowntree Foundation.

Tanner, K. and Le Riche, P. (1995) '"You see but you do not observe." The art of observation and its application to practice teaching.' *Issues in Social Work Education 15*, 2, 66–80.

Thoburn, J., Lewis, A. and Shemmings, D. (1995) *Paternalism or Partnership? Family Involvement in the Child Protection Process.* London: HMSO.

Wise, S. (1985) *Becoming a Feminist Social Worker.* Studies in Sexual Politics No.6, University of Manchester.

Wise, S. (1995) 'Feminist ethics in practice.' In R. Hugman and D. Smith (eds) *Ethical Issues in Social Work.* London and New York: Routledge.

CHAPTER THREE

A Process and an Event

The Use of Observation by Practice Assessors and Practice Teachers

Kate Leonard

Introduction

In this chapter I shall be exploring the use of observation as a tool in practice teaching.[1] Within an anti-discriminatory context I will discuss the competency framework for assessment and adult learning principles used in social work education and relate these to the theoretical models and concepts of observation. I will give practice examples and outline how to plan and negotiate observations in practice placements. This involves a hierarchy of assessed observations that may include the observation of a student's practice by a practice teacher, the observation of the practice teacher's supervision of the student and the student undertaking a series of observations of a service user (Tanner and Le Riche 1995). So, at any one time the observer may also

---

1   Phillipson (1992) makes a helpful distinction between anti-discriminatory practice and anti-oppressive practice which I shall use. I use the term anti-discriminatory because I believe that, currently, social workers and managers work within a framework where there is unfairness in the current structures of society. These need to be challenged and reformed and, eventually, restructured. When I use this term I refer to discrimination on the grounds of race, gender, disability, age, sexuality, class, religion, HIV/AIDS status. It is important to recognise that there is an inter-relationship betweendifferent areas of oppression. A multiple oppression model addresses all areas of oppression and does not create a hierarchy of oppressions. 'Anti-oppressive practice, however, works with a model of empowerment and liberation and requires a fundamental rethinking of values, institutions and relationships' (Phillipson 1992, p.15).

be the observed. This means that a culture of openness has to be encouraged in the practice placement.

The introduction in 1991 by the Central Council for Education and Training in Social Work (CCETSW) of the Diploma in Social Work (DipSW) and the Practice Teachers' Award was the result of a review of how social workers were trained and assessed.

These changes in the qualifying requirements and the introduction of formal post-qualifying awards occurred as a result of political disquiet in the mid-1980s. (Following child death enquiries, the government and media queried what social workers actually did to protect children.) The concerns were that social workers were not being trained in the rudiments of the work and did not have sufficient knowledge of the law.

These changes recognised that, previously, professional competence was accepted at the point of qualification in social work without any formal viewing of the students' practice in their work with clients/service users and that there was no process that assessed or observed a practice teacher's competence as a teacher.

The Introduction of the Competency Framework and the Use of Direct Observation

The introduction of a competency framework in social work education and the formalising of 'partnership' arrangements between placement providers and colleges in designing and agreeing the structure of the DipSW and practice teacher programmes meant that the quality of college teaching and placement learning opportunities within agencies was reviewed. It was hoped that this would lead to enhanced practice learning opportunities due to the introduction of a standardisation of the quality of service offered by practice teachers, with greater emphasis on the practice element of training and a growth in placements. There continues to be an issue regarding the number and quality of placements, which is affected by the reduction in the size of local authorities, cuts and closures in the voluntary sector and the devolving of budgets from CCETSW to DipSW programmes to pay for placements.

Another important aim of this change was that employing authorities would have a more powerful say in how training courses are delivered, ensuring that training is aligned with the needs of the economy. Inevitably, this has meant that the largest and most powerful placement providers, usually the local authorities, have the most powerful vote in the partnerships.

Smaller voluntary agencies, and their services, can be marginalised and the need to train social workers in these areas of work forgotten – for example with homeless people.

In a wider context, competence is being used as a way of systematising and rationalising the maze of different occupational qualifications and standards. This includes the formal recognition of previous work experience and learning, with the intention that social work training would be more accessible to people without formal educational qualifications through the recognition of recently introduced qualifications such as National Vocational Qualifications (NVQs) and the formal assessment of Accredited Prior Learning (APL) and Accredited Prior Experiential Learning (APEL).

Assessment through observation of a student's practice was formally introduced for the DipSW in Paper 30 (CCETSW 1989, 1991a). Observation as a method of assessment for trainee practice teachers was introduced for the first time with the introduction of the practice teachers' award outlined in papers 26.3 (CCETSW 1991b) and 26.4 (CCETSW 1996), the purpose being to improve standards of practice and service delivery provided by social workers at the point of qualification. Both requirements were introduced at the same time as the move to using the competency framework in social work education.

CCETSW requires DipSW students to be observed three times in their work with a service user in each practice placement they undertake in a social work agency. They undertake two placements – the first is for fifty days minimum and the second placement for eighty days minimum – during a two-year course. The primary purpose of these observations is to assess the student against a set of competencies – six core competencies and value requirements – that define the knowledge, skills and values the student is expected to demonstrate at the point of qualification. The practice teacher will be the main assessor of the student's practice component, although evidence may be gained from other parties.

A practice teacher undertaking the CCETSW Practice Teachers' Award course is required to take formal responsibility for a student's placement and to be observed offering supervision to the student on a minimum of two occasions. This supervision is observed by a practice assessor. CCETSW requires that the practice assessor 'will normally be a qualified social worker or allied professional with at least two years experience of practice teaching, staff supervision, post-qualifying (PQ) mentoring or teaching/assessment. It is desirable they hold the Practice Teaching Award' (CCETSW 1996). The practice teacher is assessed against a set of five competencies relating to their role. These competencies are defined by CCETSW. The practice assessor's assessment will be one element of assessment of the practice teacher's portfolio. This evidence becomes part of the overall evidence gathered from a range of methods of assessment to decide on her competency as a practice teacher.

Students on many DipSW courses also undertake a series of up to ten hour-long observations of a service user, often a child but sometimes an adult. This may or may not take place in the context of a practice placement and is an adaptation of the model developed by the Tavistock Centre (Trowell and Miles 1991) to study infant development and relationships between the child, the carers and the observer. After the visit the student records the observation in as much detail as possible. The students then take it in turns to present one of their observations and subsequent recording at a series of seminars run by the college tutors and practice teachers. This method of observation is discussed elsewhere in this book and will not be addressed here.

Looking at Competency Frameworks

In order to understand and use the competency framework in social work education, and, more specifically, how to use observation as a tool for this type of assessment, it is important for the reader to recognise that social work is one of many occupations subject to this framework of assessment. The concept of competence is constantly being developed and reviewed. As a result, there are a number of definitions from a range of training, educational and employment bodies that address the concepts of overall competence and the meeting of particular competencies within a specific work role. I want to introduce three definitions. The first two definitions are quoted by Issitt and Woodward (1992, p.46). The NCVQ provides a narrow definition of competence: 'the ability to perform work activities to the standards required in employment'. This definition is simple and does not address the complexities of the integral assessment of values, knowledge and skills and the ability to be a reflective and innovative social work practitioner.

The second is a broader definition that appears to have been widely used in the education and employment fields and provided by the Training Agency:

> Competence is defined as the ability to perform the activities within
> an occupation. Competence is a wide term which embodies the ability
> to transfer skills and knowledge to new situations within the occupa-
> tional area. It encompasses organisation and planning of work, inno-
> vation and coping with non routine activities. It includes those
> qualities of personal effectiveness that are required in the workplace
> to deal with co-workers, managers and customers.

Although a broad definition, this quotation identifies the abilities necessary
to be a competent social work practitioner. This includes the ability to
transfer learning and to be able to reflect on, adapt to and work in constantly
changing and new situations. It also includes other vital aspects of social
work, such as attention to the personal qualities necessary to the profession
and the ability to work in a team. This definition lacks any reference to how
such competence is to be assessed.

Third, Wolf (1995) outlines a definition of her own that I think is
extremely helpful. It encapsulates the process of assessment undertaken in a
competency framework and reminds assessors of the need to consider how
'clear and transparent' the defined competency requirements are in social
work education:

> Competence-based assessment is a form of assessment that is derived
> from the specification of a set of outcomes; that so clearly states both
> the outcomes – general and specific – that assessors, students and in-
> terested third parties can all make reasonably objective judgements
> with respect to student achievement or non achievement of these out-
> comes; and that certifies student progress on the basis of demon-
> strated achievement of these outcomes. Assessments are not tied to
> time served in educational settings. (p.1)

Wolf emphasises that outcomes should 'be specified to the point where they
are clear and transparent – that assessors, assessees and "third parties" should
be able to understand what is being assessed, and what should be achieved'
(p.2).

In order to decide on the required outcomes necessary for a person to be
competent in an occupation, a functional analysis of the competencies
required by many occupations has to be undertaken. The NVQ care
standards demonstrate a broad example of this analysis. The underlying
principles involve breaking down the work of a competent worker into key

roles, the main functions, or units of competence, of these roles and the elements of these functions. Criteria are then set, against which the worker's performance of the tasks will be measured.

Since 1995, with CCETSW's rewriting of the Practice Teachers' Award and DipSW, there has been greater clarity of the competency framework in social work education. There is now more emphasis on national agreed standards and a move away from each college interpreting the competencies in their own style, as was the case with the introduction of the DipSW and practice teaching awards in 1991. Both awards now emphasise the demonstration and integration of social work values and knowledge within the competency framework. There are also crucial references to the student and practice teacher being able to reflect and critically analyse their practice and identify, use and transfer knowledge skills and values in practice.

The current application by CCETSW (1995) of the competency framework to training in the social work profession defines six core competencies and underlying value requirements that define the purpose of social work role:

1. Communicate and engage

2. Promote and enable

3. Assess and plan

4. Intervene and provide services

5. Work in organisations

6. Develop professional competence.

Value Requirements:

- Identify and question their own values and prejudices, and their implications for practice

- respect and value uniqueness and diversity, and recognise and build on strengths

- promote people's rights to choice, privacy, confidentiality and protection, while recognising and addressing the complexities of competing rights and demands

- assist people to increase control of and improve the quality of their lives, while recognising that control of behaviour will be required at times in order to protect children and adults from harm

- identify, analyse and take action to counter discrimination, racism, disadvantage, inequality and injustice, using strategies appropriate to role and context
- practice in a manner that does not stigmatise or disadvantage either individuals, groups or communities.

Within each core competency there are a varying number of practice requirements. Each practice requirement lists examples of evidence indicators. It is against each practice requirement that the practice teacher must identify and measure evidence of competence.

For practice teachers, five units of competence are identified:

- Unit A: Values
- Unit B: Management
- Unit C: Teaching
- Unit D: Assessment
- Unit E: Reflective practice.

Under each of these units are a varying number of elements of competence against which the practice teacher is assessed.

The Use of the Competency Framework in Assessment

There are a range of debates about the introduction of competency-led vocational training and its benefits and suitability to professional training courses such as social work. Central to the debate about the usefulness of the competency framework for assessment in the social work profession has to be how it incorporates anti-discriminatory practice. It was expected that one of the benefits of a more detailed competency schedule would be that there would be a reduction in the potential for subjectivity and discrimination in the assessment process. Issitt and Woodward (1992) outline the theoretical model of the competency framework, which is positivist and behavioural in its origins. They argue that person-centred professionals' work roles have been broken down into a number of individualistic and mechanistic tasks carried out in isolation and that this can hide structural issues of oppression that social workers and other care professionals need to address. They also argue that a competency method of assessment focuses purely on outcomes. There is no room for assessors to measure, in a holistic way, the person's developing professional ability, which is seen to be something more than the sum of the competency requirements and includes an ability to work in an anti-discriminatory way, to be trustworthy, analytic, reflective and innovatory. The experiential models of teaching and learning traditionally used in many colleges of further and higher education offering vocational training pay attention to the process of learning, as well as the outcome, at discrete points of assessment. It is important that a person has an in-depth understanding of why and how they demonstrated the required outcomes and can justify these. Central to these experiential models are the principles of adult learning described by Knowles (1972), the concept of the reflective practitioner as outlined by Schön (1983) and the importance of experiential learning as defined by Kolb (1993) in a model that emphasises the need to develop four different types of abilities: concrete experience, reflective observation, abstract conceptualisation and active experimentation.

Yelloly (1995) and Jones and Joss (1995) state that a holistic approach to training and assessment that incorporates the model of the reflective practitioner is necessary and that this can be integrated into a competency framework. They argue that in order to be competent, social workers must become reflective practitioners. The assessment of professional competence inevitably has to address the cognitive process that occurs when a person is gaining knowledge, values and skills in order for the assessor to know whether she understands why a particular outcome was seen to be evidence of competency and another to be insufficient evidence or even evidence of bad practice.

Likewise, in my view, a competent practice teacher must be able to identify the reflective practitioner within herself and learn how to teach this professional framework to the student, while recognising that we all learn in different ways.

However, these models, alongside the general competency model, lack any explicit discussion of anti-discriminatory practice and how to provide an environment for experiential learning that is conducive to every learner. Humphries (1988) outlines very clearly how education institutions offering learning opportunities cannot be seen as a neutral environment and she makes suggestions for change. The recognition of different life experiences and the effect of racism, heterosexism, classism, sexism and disablism in the education system can halt learners from these oppressed groups from fulfilling their potential in formal educational systems. It is, therefore, important to focus on the process of teaching the student in the best way possible in order to assist positive outcomes at the points of assessment.

Humphries (1988, pp.14–15) suggests three 'basic principles of a value base towards liberation':

1. An acknowledgement of the relationship between major social divisions in society. In educational practice this means an awareness of the limits of self direction and choice for some students because of the distribution of power, the way this is maintained through socially ascribed and apparently fixed roles and relationships rooted in institutionalised ideologies.

2. To make links between personal and political processes, particularly as these are mediated through the 'hidden curriculum'. This means widening the range of experiences seen as legitimate as prior learning and as a basis for future learning.

3. To use educational methods which have as central the notion of 'empowerment', involving working for the redistribution of power in education through the recruitment of people from oppressed groups, both as students and staff; through resisting labelling of students; through the structuring of learning that gives oppressed minorities a voice; through adopting more appropriate assessment criteria; through opening up learning programmes to the scrutiny of black communities; and through planning of other strategies towards change.

Competency-based assessment in social work initially allowed each college considerable freedom in interpreting and developing the competency framework for practice placements. Subsequently, competency frameworks have been rewritten and refined (CCETSW 1995, 1996). The current requirements for both the DipSW and the Practice Teachers' Award demonstrate a continued, systematic development of the use of a competency framework, demonstrating in a more explicit way the links between knowledge, skills and values and providing more specific assessment criteria that can be used universally by colleges.

However, the broad core competencies for both social work awards discussed in this chapter are problematic in that they cannot assume an objective reality. The competencies for the qualification in social work are particularly broad in recognition that social work occurs in a range of statutory, voluntary and private agencies carrying out a range of tasks with different emphases depending on the agency and legal requirements. Assessment is a subjective process. In reality, therefore, practice teachers and practice assessors have to make interpretations as to what is deemed competent in a particular context. For example, the practice competency requirements for both awards do not explicitly include linking theory and practice, although one can assume it is essential and, therefore, incorporate it into most of the requirements.

Wolf (1995) writes widely about the use of competence-led assessment in a variety of occupations. This is relevant to social work education in that she makes a clear statement that the broader the concept of what competence involves, the more likely there is to be a variety of standards of assessment. She takes a pragmatic approach to the understanding and interpretation of the competency-led framework, arguing that competence is a construct in the same way knowledge is. Competence and knowledge can both be measured by behavioural indicators. Assessors of competency still have to make complex judgements, as do academics in examination assessment. She argues that in order for the system to identify competence and 'for the system to deliver on its promises, this domain needs to be specified in such a clear and unambiguous way that anyone involved in assessment will know exactly "what to do"' (p.55). She outlines two major issues that have a direct impact on the way assessors operate: the inherently high variability in the context of assessment and the way in which assessments and evidence are aggregated to reach a final judgement about whether competence has been achieved.

Wolf talks about how 'assessors do not simply match candidates behaviour to assessment instructions in a mechanistic fashion'. Instead, experienced assessors

> operate in terms of an internalised, holistic set of concepts about what an assessment 'ought' to show, and about how, and how far, they can take account of the context of the performance, make allowances, refer to other evidence about the candidate in deciding 'what they really meant'. The internalised model of competence may or may not reflect other assessors or the course expectations (1995, p.67).

It is important to locate these debates about subjectivity and the striving for objectivity in assessment in an overriding framework of anti-discriminatory practice. This debate needs to recognise the range of perspectives in the profession as well as the strength of dominant perspectives. The unequal power relationships within society and organisations – such as local authorities and colleges, the managers, practice assessors, practice teachers, students and service users/clients – cannot be ignored. For example, an agency where a student is on placement will have an organisational or team view of what they see as evidence of the competent social worker. This may differ from the college view or another agency view. It is important that regulatory mechanisms for the assessment process are in place. For example, assessment panels and exam boards will monitor standards of student placement reports and practice teacher portfolios.

Measuring Competency

Fawcett (1996) refers to a checklist model as a scientific form of child observation where the observer ticks off behaviour as part of a developmental assessment of a young child. Linking this to the notion of competency discussed earlier, the observer is again faced with the notion of how much of the behaviour is necessary to deem a student or practice teacher competent. If the observer just ticks the box, a third person does not know what prompted the tick unless a description is provided. Inevitably, the description provided is the summary of a complex process of observation and assessment. It is important for the observer, as practice assessor or practice teacher, to consider before the assessment what and how much evidence of each competency can be provided from the observation and what is deemed acceptable in terms of depth of evidence. The Practice Teachers' Award courses and DipSW courses should provide training and support and formal structures for regulating and monitoring the standards of evidence expected. Evidence can be collected in a variety of ways:

- direct observation
- written evidence, such as supervision notes and reports, and contracts
- discussions before and after the observation that provide secondary evidence
- responses to, and use of, feedback.

The observer has to consider how much weight to give to evidence provided in these various ways. Is one sentence about 'anti-racism' enough or one reference to theory? How do you measure whether these issues are fully integrated? For example, evidence of anti-discriminatory practice and the linking of theory and practice needs to be provided in all these ways to demonstrate to the observer that these aspects are integrated consistently into the placement. A depth of understanding has to be demonstrated and a one-off sentence or acknowledgement is not sufficient. Current debate includes the need to provide evidence of a range of oppressions. The use of a grid with the terms fully met, partially met and not met are useful ways of recording evidence against each competency in written feedback from the observer, with comments and suggestions as to how to meet the competency in the next observation or through other evidence – for example reports.

The Use of Observation as a Tool for Assessment Within the Competency Framework

Kemshall (1993) argues that assessment cannot be value free and that there are competing forces deciding the importance of each competency in specific agencies – for example college, CCETSW, statutory and voluntary agencies – or among different groups of professionals involved in the assessment – for example tutor, student, practice teacher, practice assessor. If an assumption is made that this process is value free, this ignores the impact of a dominant perspective that inevitably oppresses other minority views. She points out that the competency framework is designed in a white, eurocentric, male framework similar to many of the large institutions and influential and powerful voices in this society. While recognising that it was hoped that a clearer framework using direct observational evidence would reduce possible discrimination, she fears it will drive discrimination underground. She calls for clear training in anti-discriminatory practice; that the core competencies and assessment reflect anti-discriminatory practice, consider the issues of line managers as assessors, offer support and mentoring for black workers and women and ensure assessment boards are made up of people from a diverse range of backgrounds – for example race, gender, sexuality, disability, class, age. The use of the general term 'anti-discriminatory' practice in itself allows the range of oppressions to go unnamed and can lead to the assessment process failing to focus on the range of interconnected oppressions. In order to demonstrate competence, the student should use a multiple oppression model and be expected to give specific examples of their practice.

O'Hagan (1996), arguing from a different perspective, sees this view as outdated and unresearched and asserts that the most recent CCETSW Paper 30 requirements for the DipSW has a core competence 'work in organisations' that attempts 'to influence the organisational collective of which the student is a part towards upholding clients rights and combating discriminatory and oppressive practice' (p.18). Likewise, one could assume that the value requirements of the DipSW should perpetuate anti-discriminatory practice, as do the Practice Teacher Award value requirements.

O'Hagan (1996) does not address how to teach and assess the levels of personal change that need to occur to develop an awareness and subsequent ability to make active, anti-discriminatory professional interventions. Nor does he appear to understand the importance of making explicit links between the macro context of anti-discriminatory legislation, policy and procedure and how these are, in reality, put into practice at a micro level when observation is used as a tool for assessment. It is the detail of the interactions between service users, clients, students, practice teachers and practice assessors that predominantly occur behind closed doors. In order to place this model of assessment in an anti-discriminatory context, it is very important to address the detail of these interactions, the power dynamics at play and the personal and professional value and knowledge base of all involved. This should be set in an organisational culture of anti-discriminatory practice where individual workers are trained to have a professional responsibility to address such issues in their own practice, to teach the student or practice teacher best practice and in challenging team members and the larger organisation. This encourages a bottom-up approach, as well as top-down approach, that is necessary for organisations to work in an anti-discriminatory way.

I am, therefore, more reticent in my belief that the competency framework will enforce anti-discriminatory practice in the use of observation without the commitment of individual students, practice teachers and practice assessors, tutors, external examiners and programme directors to put anti-discriminatory practice into the broad competency framework. In order to work to a common understanding of what is seen as a competent practice teacher or social worker at point of qualification, there needs to be consistency in the assessment process. Assessment by observation is one method of assessment within this process. In order to regulate standards within DipSW, practice teaching programmes and nationally, there are mechanisms in place to check that standards are consistent – for example training and monitoring in the use of observation and the employment of external examiners and assessment panels to read practice teachers' reports within each programme.

Models of Observation

Practice assessors, practice teachers and students need to have an understanding of the range of models of observation. The importance of the use of observation in the development of good social work practice has been written about by a number of authors (McMahon and Farnfield 1994; Trowell and Miles 1991; Wilson 1992). Initially, this focused on the observation of young children in a training model developed by the Tavistock Clinic. More recently, observation has been undertaken in colleges with students observing children, families and adults, and organisations and in practice teaching. Other models of observation are referred to in other chapters in this book – for example in family therapy work. The format for observation in practice teaching has a distinct model of its own.

Both Fawcett (1996) and Le Riche and Tanner (1996) identify two broad approaches – the scientific/sampling methods and the narrative methods – to the purpose of observation. They stem from different theoretical perspectives and have different purposes.

Le Riche and Tanner outline four strands important to the narrative model:

- reality is a personal construct and is determined by what the observer sees

- the construction of this reality will be affected by what the observer sees as important and what s/he can tolerate

- value is placed on the context of the observed. Detailed and specific behaviours are considered in terms of their meaning within the overall context of the person observed

- the observation is then described in a written report and its ensuing status and meaning given by different parties reading the report.

Rather than observe every detail memorable, the scientific model of observation is interested in observing and recording in an objective way a range of specific behaviours that are pre-selected and may be dependent on a particular time and place.

Tanner (Chapter Two) discusses a third model called the Equality Model of observation (see also Le Riche and Tanner 1996). Tanner argues that the scientific and narrative models do not address issues of power and inequality and 'that observation has an important role to play in social work education and practice but if it is to be effective and congruent with social work values then it needs to put at its centre issues of power and difference'. Her model draws from critical social policy and the realist model in social science. It sets the experience of being observed within the context of personal experience and structural inequalities perpetuated through organisational, social and political structures. She raises principles of partnership, client/service user involvement and ownership of written material in a discussion about negotiation and recording of the observational process and the need for the observer to reflect critically on her abilities in the role of observer, her personal and professional values and knowledge and skill base.

In an earlier article, Tanner and Le Riche (1995) refer to Murrell's description of two phases of observational judgement. The 'process stage' where 'the vast amount of data which is bombarding an individual is sifted and placed by the observer in categories', they see as vital in allowing the observer to reflect on what she observes before 'imposing theoretical perspectives or rushing into premature judgements'. They use the metaphor of the filter as a way of thinking about how information gained through observation can be managed and structured. The second is the 'inference stage'. This 'involves using the data which is accepted and recorded to make a meaningful interpretation of "reality" and evaluations' (p.68).

These two phases are helpful when considering the role of the observational process in practice teaching. Inevitably, as the observation, either of practice or supervision, is part of an assessment of competency, observers need to match what they observe against a set of CCETSW competencies and to analyse this process both during and after the session. In addition, there is a third stage where the assessor gives direct feedback verbally and in writing. This means that observation is not naturalistic in the true sense as it is planned beforehand. The observed person is briefed as to what is expected of them within the context of the process of offering a social work service or practice teaching a student. They know the assessment criteria and need to consider how they are demonstrating these. This type of observation is truly purposeful as defined by Le Riche in the observational matrix described in Chapter One. The minimum of three observations of a student's practice and of two observed sessions for the Practice Teachers' Award offers the observer an opportunity of a number of snapshots over time of the student's practice and practice teacher's supervision. These observations provide cumulative observed evidence of competence, so avoiding a one-off 'performance' of good practice. They also allow time for the student or practice teacher to reflect on the feedback from previous observations in order to demonstrate in depth competence over time and the ability to learn and develop new skills. As new evidence is gained alongside existing evidence, including written reports, the assessor is more able to gain an overview of whether or not good practice skills are developing.

An observation model for practice teaching is based fully within the Equality Model, given the value and knowledge base of social work education. This model takes strands from the scientific model through the provision, by CCETSW, of specific measurable competencies that the observer looks for in the limited time available. The student or practice teacher's practice is measured against these in the observation, almost like a checklist. The use of the narrative model in practice teaching recognises the importance of the personal construction of reality and the impact on the process of observation for the observed and the observer and the implications for subjectivity by the assessor.

The Use of Recorded Observation Agreements

It is important to consider the impact the observer has on the process she is observing. The person who is going to be observed may understandably feel nervous and, ideally, the series of observations should begin when the student or practice teacher to be observed has had a chance to gain some confidence in her role. The practice teacher and practice assessor, as observer, have a major role in managing the climate and structure of the observation and that is why it is so important to address the power dynamics of the negotiation. The practice teacher may assist the student by arranging for the student to observe her practice first. The power dynamics must be explored and the practice assessor and practice teacher, in their role as observer, must take responsibility for modelling how to do this. As part of a formal agreement to work together, they need to discuss:

- the independent role of the observer
- their own professional values and anti-discriminatory practices and the impact of personal values on the development of these
- their own experience and/or knowledge of oppression and anti-discriminatory practice. We all will be at differing levels in different areas and will continue to learn about our practice – for example race, gender, class, disability, lesbian and gay issues, age
- the relevant legislative framework

- the impact of organisational policy and practice on their relationship
- commonalities and differences in order to avoid oppressive assumptions and stereotypes.

Recognition of commonalities and differences regarding depth of, or lack of, experience and/or knowledge regarding anti-discriminatory practice allow a basis for each party to learn and change. Knowledge and awareness is not a static process, it is variable and ever changing and it continues through our careers as long as we are open to this possibility and prepared to take risks. This process has to be set in the context of power differentials in the practice teaching relationship. It is the observer's responsibility to lead this discussion by talking about their own values and anti-discriminatory practice, to set up a climate of trust and openness and independently assess their own abilities in relation to anti-discriminatory practice as well as those of the person they are assessing. Each practice teacher–student–client–practice assessor relationship will have its own power base. It is important to recognise who holds the power in relation to whom. For example, the practice teacher has power within the relationship to pass or fail the student. The student has power over the service offered to the service user. If the practice teacher is a black woman, the student a white man and the service user a white woman, this has to be set in the context of the potential for racism and sexism from the student and service user. If the male student is gay and the practice teacher and practice assessor are heterosexual, the impact of potential heterosexism for the student needs to be included in the service user–student–practice teacher dynamic.

It is important not to make assumptions about similarities between, for example, two white workers or two black workers. The observer needs to discuss commonalities and differences in relation to culture, gender, class, sexuality and disability. For example, it is oppressive to assume that the student is heterosexual or that the practice teacher does not have a disability. It is also important to avoid collusion in choosing to ignore an oppression, as in the case of two white male workers not addressing issues of racism or sexism.

These dynamics need to be discussed explicitly. That is not to say that only the oppressions relevant to the people involved should be acknowledged, they all should, but these are particularly relevant to these relationships and will provide a bridge to discussing and learning about anti-discriminatory social work practice in a broader context. It is also important not to use the power as observer in an abusive way that exploits the practice teacher or student. For example, asking them to teach the observer about their experience of oppression or expecting them to answer as a spokesperson for everyone experiencing that particular oppression. It is necessary to accept that the student or practice teacher may know more than the observer at times. However, the boundary between exploitation and exchange is narrow and the observer must consider how she is going to take responsibility for her lack of knowledge and experience, perhaps through organising her own consultancy or supervision.

Identifying the competencies to be assessed through the work observed can also help the person being observed to feel more empowered in what can be an anxiety-provoking situation. Expectations need to be clear and in Appendix 1 of this chapter I outline suggested headings for a written agreement concerning the role of the practice assessor when observing the practice teacher. The agreement is between practice assessor, practice teacher, student and line manager. Direct observation must also be included in the student's overall learning contract, with details of its use as a method of assessment, how often and when in the placement. The practice teacher needs to consider the type of observation – for example an interview with a client/family, presentation at a conference or team meeting, or running a group. This decision will partly be made on the competencies the practice teacher wants to see evidence of. These need to be clearly contracted and the purpose and plan for the interview discussed in detail in supervision. The observer must agree when and if they will intervene. I find it helpful to reassure the student that I will intervene if the interview is unhelpful to the client/service user – for example giving major pieces of wrong information or advice. This assists them in knowing that the interview is going reasonably well if no intervention by the observer is made. If an interview or supervision session does not go to plan, this can cause anxiety for both student and practice teacher.

Students are often unable to realise that a flexibility of approach to working with clients and an ability to deal with what is presented is part of being a competent, reflective practitioner – for example if there is a crisis, they need to be able to reassess, review, engage and make new plans. It is also important that they maintain a focus that addresses their responsibilities as a worker for the agency. Other issues to be considered are the use of service user feedback in the assessment process, time to give immediate verbal feedback and to follow up with written feedback and evidence of competencies not met, part met or fully met. Detailed guidelines are included as an appendix in the article by Tanner and Le Riche (1995).

The use of an agreement makes explicit to all parties the roles and responsibilities of those involved. This acknowledges that the observer will have an impact on the parties being observed, however inactive they appear during the observation. My presence as a practice assessor observing practice teachers has had notable impacts – for example with the student being on her best behaviour in order to help the practice teacher 'pass' or using the opportunity to confront the practice teacher about their discriminatory behaviour towards them with someone else present to witness and assess the practice teacher's ability to face the challenge.

Impact of the Observation on the Observer

The process of the observation will also have an impact on the observer. The observer, whether it be practice teacher or practice assessor, will have to consider the impact of the process of observing on herself and have sufficient skills to recognise, manage and analyse her own feelings and thoughts about the experience of being the observer. She needs to make sure she has time to reflect on the experience of observing, to seek supervision or consultancy as necessary, to filter information and provide clear evidence of whether each competency has been met fully, partially or not at all and to incorporate this in the verbal and subsequent written feedback to the person observed. If the observer is finding a situation uncomfortable – for example silence, crying, shouting – she may have an overpowering wish to intervene in order to put an end to these feelings. Alternatively, the observer may ignore and block-off from the process, perhaps by concentrating on taking notes on other areas for the use of feedback after the observation. Other examples of feelings that become evident in the role of observer are those of boredom, enjoyment, excitement, frustration and impatience.

The purpose of intervention by the observer during an observation – for example the risk to a service user/client, the provision of wrong information or abuse of the client during an observation – needs to be discussed in the agreement in order to avoid an unwelcome interruption that might undermine the practice teacher or student when it is not necessary. The focus of the observation is for assessment purposes and, therefore, time has to be provided where the practice teacher or student provide evidence, whether it be sufficient or not, without the help of the observer to make the evidence better or good enough through 'coaching' or intervening. An observation is one event in the process of several observations used for assessment purposes. In this respect, the observation cannot be treated in the same way as live supervision, joint work or co-work where a shared responsibility or immediate intervention is made to assist the person being observed. This is because the aim is to provide evidence of competence at this point in time and identify future teaching and learning required in order to achieve full competence at the end of the observations/course.

Observation Triangles and Hierarchies of Observation

Mattinson (Mattinson and Sinclair 1979) identifies 'the reflection process in casework supervision' and focuses on the supervisory triangle made up of the client, the worker and the supervisor. She describes how the client–worker relationship can affect the supervisory relationship and that the person in the triangle causing the most anxiety is the one likely to be excluded by the others in the triangle. She introduces the idea that 'the responses of workers which are out of character with their normal behaviour and which are defensive in quality give an important indication of the strength and type of disturbance to which they have been subjected' (p.56).

I have found it important to examine the hierarchies, context and dynamics of the triads that operate in practice teaching, particularly in relation to direct observations. In an observation of a practice teacher's supervision session, the student, the practice teacher and practice assessor form a triad. The concept of the reflection process can be used when considering the triangular supervisory relationships for the client–student–practice teacher and the student–practice teacher–practice assessor. It is important for the observer to make sure they are not colluding with one another against the third person – for example practice teacher and student against the client, student and practice assessor against the practice teacher. The behaviours stemming from such alliances are those of ignoring the failing competencies in the assessment process, focusing only on the strengths, not being prepared or able to challenge or only recognising weaknesses and not strengths in a person. Kadushin (1968), in his article about 'games people play in supervision', provides a useful introduction to help the observer consider her role and avoid introducing games herself or contributing to any games being played out in the supervisory relationship either by colluding with the student or practice teacher. The article addresses issues in relation to the expected losses and demands placed on both parties in such a relationship and how games are enacted through avoiding disagreements and attempting to change the unequal power relationships without explicitly discussing these issues.

The observer has a key task of identifying such a process and deciding what action to take and how to contain these feelings and make a useful intervention to explore a hypothesis in the feedback session. When entering into Murrell's second inference stage, I think the observer needs to consider using a range of theoretical perspectives that explain anti-discriminatory theory and practice and the internal and external world. The observer needs to identify explicitly how they use these theories to analyse this process. For example, the notion of the 'reflection process' derives from the psychoanalytic thinking of the Tavistock Clinic. The Equality Model evolved by Le Riche and Tanner (1996) addresses the power dynamics in the practice teaching relationship. Issues of power must be addressed as part of any hypothesis about the reflection process, or the games played, in order to avoid the increased potential for oppressive behaviours by the observer.

Example of the Contracting of an Observation by a Practice Assessor

I am observing a practice teacher on three occasions supervising a student. In our initial agreement session I have asked the practice teacher to spend 30–45 minutes of the second observed session teaching the student about an area of social work practice that links theory and practice and is set within an anti-discriminatory framework. This allows plenty of planning time for the practice teacher to discuss with the student a useful topic and also introduces this task as a routine part of supervision that is not just carried out for my benefit and then forgotten. I expect evidence of these areas in both observations but this task offers a clear structure as it will also give me specific evidence of a number of competencies all at once and in depth in a short period of time – for example Elements of Units A, B and C for the Practice Teachers' Award (CCETSW 1995). My aim is to introduce a layered approach to measuring competency and through introducing this task I want to see the practice teacher's ability to:

- plan learning opportunities
- use supervision time effectively and have a clear agenda and structure to the session
- use a range of teaching methods apart from case discussion
- apply theory to the student's work with clients/service users

- to critique theory in an anti-discriminatory framework
- address the power dynamics at play in the interaction between the student and practice teacher.

I expect practice teachers to keep to an agenda but if the student is distressed, renegotiation is important. Rigidly pursuing the original agenda can be punitive and I would not see this as a competent way of addressing the situation. The practice teacher needs to keep in mind the personal professional boundaries agreed in the contract and the practice teacher–student role.

When asked to do this, practice teachers' initial fears relate to having to deliver a lecture and not having a sufficient knowledge base. I think it is important as a practice assessor to facilitate practice teachers to think about their role. They need to consider how they address their feelings, review their knowledge base, facilitate the student's learning and how they demonstrate this to the practice assessor. For example:

- Encouragement to consider a range of teaching methods, such as both reading a book or article about task-centred practice and discussing the application, its role in anti-discriminatory practice and its benefits and drawbacks to work with a particular service user/client.

- The use of brainstorming as a teaching method to assess the strengths and risks in relation to the client or service user with whom the student is working. The black strengths model as outlined by Ahmed (1990) and Macdonald (1991) outlines good practice for assessing black families within an anti-racist framework. It emphasises a balanced assessment that identifies strengths and difficulties but does not pathologise or stereotype black families. The model can be used as a basis for working in a broader anti-discriminatory framework and is equally relevant for practitioners working with adults.

- Asking the student to draw a family tree using a genogram and considering the family dynamics, extended family members' roles.

- Designing a brief case study with questions for the student to answer. These can, for example, relate to identifying the legislation used, identifying the detail of how the student worked in an anti-discriminatory framework, identifying plans and decisions made. The student can be given the task to complete before supervision and the practice teacher can then focus on relevant learning points in the supervision session.

These, and many more interactive adult learning techniques, are often preferable to a didactic lecture. At times, information giving is necessary and helpful. It demonstrates the practice teacher's knowledge base in a chosen subject, which is an important aspect of her competence, but she also needs to demonstrate an ability to facilitate the student's own thoughts, reflections and learning in line with the notion of the reflective practitioner outlined earlier in the discussion of adult learning principles. Pacing is very important here. The practice teacher needs to remember that a student learning new information and skills will need time to integrate this into her practice. The practice teacher may well need to be reminded to make the link between adult learning principles and the student's learning process. Reynolds (1949) outlines such a process. The practice teacher is now at the fifth stage of learning to teach what she is competent in social work practice. The knowledge, values and skills she acquired some time ago have been fully integrated. A student will need to go through the first four stages in learning identified by Reynolds, ranging from acute consciousness of self to 'relative mastery', probably at some point after qualification. This learning process can be facilitated by the practice teacher through the use of open questions and setting tasks, both in preparation for and during supervision, that encourage the student to take responsibility for herself and reflect on her own practice. A practice teacher's ability to teach and offer guidance through a dialogue with the student about practice, rather than embark on a road of telling the student what to do, is a very important part of the process of learning for the student and of becoming an effective practice teacher. It is important for a practice teacher to think about how the student learns best and to use a variety of methods of teaching in supervision about an area before assessing the student as failing.

Assessment of the student is an ongoing process throughout the placement, but there are also particular points or events where an assessment is made against the competency framework. These points are usually the three direct observations, the mid-way and final reports stages. This teaching process has to be set in the context of agency policy and procedure and not offer clients/service users an inadequate or discriminatory service, or put them at risk of abuse by professionals or others, at the expense of the students learning.

Conclusion

Through discussion of the observer role of the practice teacher and practice assessor, I have addressed the process and depth of assessment of competence, the developments in anti-discriminatory practice and how the competencies are interpreted, monitored and standardised. Clients and service users are expected to talk openly to social workers about themselves. Students are expected to be open and have their practice observed by their practice teachers and tutors. Practice teachers are expected to be open through observation and supervision about their work too. Feedback from tutors, practice teachers and service users is positively asked for and used to assess students and practice teachers. If this process is to be seen as congruent, the power dynamics and issues of oppression must be explicitly explored between the parties and be integral to the use of observation in assessment. All parties must be open to observation, scrutiny and accountability for the service they offer. This includes managers, practice assessors, consultants, mentors and tutors as they all contribute to service delivery in social work.

References

Ahmed, B. (1990) *Black Perspectives in Social Work*. Birmingham: Venture Press.

CCETSW (1989, 1991a, 1995) *Rules and Requirements for the Diploma in Social Work*. London: CCETSW.

CCETSW (1991b) *Improving Standards in Practice Learning Paper 26.3*. London: CCETSW.

CCETSW (1996) *Rules and Requirements for the Practice Teaching Award Paper 26.4*. London: CCETSW.

Fawcett, M. (1996) *Learning Through Child Observation*. London: Jessica Kingsley Publishers.

Humphries, B. (1988) 'Adult learning in social work education: towards liberation or domestication?' *Critical Social Policy 23*, 8–21.

Issitt, M. and Woodward, M. (1992) 'Competence and contradiction.' In P. Carter, T. Jeffs and M.K. Smith (eds) *Changing Social Work and Welfare*. Buckingham: Open University Press.

Jones, S. and Joss, R. (1995) 'Models of professionalism.' In M. Yelloly and M. Henkel (eds) *Learning and Teaching in Social Work Towards Reflective Practice*. London: Jessica Kingsley Publishers.

Kadushin, A. (1968) 'Games people play in supervision.' *Social Work, USA 13*, 3, 23–32.

Kemshall, H. (1993) 'Assessing competence: scientific process or subjective inference? Do we really see it?' *Social Work Education 12*, 1, 36–45.

Knowles, M.S. (1972) 'Innovations in teaching styles and approaches bases on adult learning.' *Journal of Education for Social Work C.S.W.E.*, 8, 2, 32–39.

Kolb, D.A. (1993) 'The process of experiential learning.' In M. Thorpe, R. Edwards and A. Hanson (eds) *Culture and Processes of Adult Learning*. Buckingham: Open University Press.

Le Riche, P. and Tanner, K. (1996) 'The way forward: developing an equality model of observation for social work education and practice.' *Issues in Social Work Education 16*, 2, 3–14.

Macdonald, S. (ed) (1991) *All Equal under the Act: A Practical Guide for the Children Act 1989 for Social Workers*. London: Race Equality Unit.

Mattinson, J. and Sinclair, I. (1979) *Mate and Stalemate*. Oxford: Blackwell.

McMahon, L. and Farnfield, S. (1994) 'Infant and child observation as preparation for social work practice.' *Social Work Education 13*, 3, 81–99.

O'Hagan, K. (ed) (1996) *Competence in Social Work Practice: A Guide for Professionals*. London: Jessica Kingsley Publishers.

Phillipson, J. (1992) *Practicing Equality Women Men and Social Work*. London: CCETSW.

Reynolds, B. (1949) *Learning and Teaching in the Practice of Social Work*. New York: Rinehart and Co.

Schön, D. (1983) *The Reflective Practitioner: How Professionals Think in Action*. New York: Basic Books.

Tanner, K. and Le Riche, P. (1995) 'You see but you do not observe. The art of observation and its application to practice teaching.' *Issues in Social Work Education 15*, 2, 66–80.

Trowell, J. and Miles, G. (1991) 'The contribution of observation training to professional development in social work.' *Journal of Social Work Practice 5*, 1, 51–60.

Wilson, K. (1992) 'The place of observation in social work training.' *Journal of Social Work Practice 6*, 1, 37–47.

Wolf, A. (1995) *Competence Based Assessment*. Buckingham: Open University Press.

Yelloly, M. (1995) 'Professional competence in higher education.' In M. Yelloly and M. Henkel (eds) *Learning and Teaching in Social Work Towards Reflective Practice*. London: Jessica Kingsley Publishers.

Acknowledgements

I would like to thank Sharon Chandler for introducing the idea of asking a practice teacher to provide a focused teaching slot in the observed supervision session.

Agreement Between Practice Assessor, Practice Teacher, Student and Line Manager

Agreement Meeting

Purpose

To clarify roles and responsibilities in relation to the work of the practice assessor and the requirements for the practice teacher of the Practice Teachers' Award course. To decide if the practice teacher and practice assessor can work together.

Observations

- Number and dates and agreement to notify of cancellation.
- Length of observed session, pre-meeting and feedback time.
- Use of feedback from the student and how this will occur.
- Agree how the practice assessor will feedback on whether requirements are being met, partially met or not met at all.
- How will the practice assessor record, both in the session and for feedback purposes?
- What evidence will the practice assessor use (e.g. observations, reports, contracts, support sessions)?
- Agree dates for practice assessors' reports and agree they will give specific evidence and a recommendation in line with the college and CCETSW requirements.
- Expectation of evidence from observations and how these relate to units and elements of competence for the award – for example Units A,B,C:
  1. Managing the structure of the session.
  2. The ability to provide learning opportunities.
  3. Anti-discriminatory practice – power differentials in practice teaching relationships, in work with clients/service users, policy and practice, linking of theory to practice.
  4. Evidence of teaching skills and use of adult learning principles.
  5. Ability to link theory and practice in depth.

- Will the practice assessor offer other help and support through additional sessions or telephone contact?
- What other tasks does the practice teacher need to undertake for the course? How does the role of the practice assessor link to these tasks?

Anti-Discriminatory Practice

- Include agreement to work together within this framework.
- Define oppressions explicitly – for example race, gender, sexuality, disability, age, class, religion, HIV/AIDS status.
- To address anti-discriminatory practice in all supervision sessions and recognise and explicitly address the power differentials existing in the practice teaching and service user relationship.
- To agree to recognise commonalities and differences between parties, to be open to discussion and challenge.
- To avoid assumptions and stereotyping.

Confidentiality

- All reports and case studies to be anonymised.
- Who the practice assessor will discuss sessions with – for example for consultancy and support.
- Who the practice teacher will discuss sessions with in line with student and client confidentiality and professional practice.

Line Management Responsibility

- Introduce the line manager to everyone involved.
- Include them in part of the agreement meeting.
- Does this remain with the line manager, practice teacher and student?
- What is the practice assessor's role in this?

The Student

- Introduce the student to everyone involved.
- Discuss the agreement with them, roles and responsibilities, the purpose of observations by the practice assessor and include them in part of the agreement meeting.
- Discuss the need for the practice assessor to read contracts and reports, include the role of the practice assessor in the student contract.
- Talk about the student's role in giving feedback.

SIGNATURE OF ALL PARTIES AND DATE.

CHAPTER FOUR

Observing the Unthinkable in Residential Care for Children

John Simmonds

The model of observation that I am drawing on in this chapter is rooted in the observation of babies and young children and developed principally at the Tavistock Clinic (Bick 1964; Brafman 1988). It is a model that has been used extensively in the training of child and other analytically orientated psychotherapists (Miller *et al.* 1989). In recent years it has been used successfully in training social workers (Pietroni 1991; Trowell 1991; Trowell and Miles 1991). While with social workers the intensity and length of the observations have been considerably reduced, the observation settings have largely remained faithful to the original theme – that of infants, young children and their carers. The advantages of observing these particular groups are clear. As this book illustrates, the power of the method has much to offer in other settings or with people at different stages in the life cycle. However, to date, little of this work, where it has been developed, has been documented. Therefore, we have limited knowledge of what is learnt when the method of observation is used beyond its original frame. Similarly, while the argument for the use of the method of observation as an important tool in the development of social workers has been well made, the use of what is learnt from observation in practice settings where social workers are engaged in routine activities related to their role and responsibilities is not well documented. This chapter is intended to address both of these issues. As such, it will explore my own experiences of using the 'observer' part of myself in settings where I had a specific role as consultant to staff groups in residential children's establishments. What was observed, therefore, was generated by adults who have primary responsibility for the care of children and young people in a setting where these professionals come together in a group to explore and think about the impact of the work on them.

I have been frequently struck, in undertaking tutorials with students beginning both qualifying and post-qualifying training, how often, while having a sense of themselves as doing a thoughtful and useful job, they feel they have had little time to think about what they are doing, particularly the impact that the work has had on them emotionally. The demands of the 'me in role' for any professional – responding, acting and communicating in complex events and circumstances – do not seem to require the explicit presence of a 'me' that is observing from a meta position what I am doing. It seems possible to act, and act responsibly, without necessarily reflecting on this from the outside. This does not seem to mean that professionals are unaware whether they have done a good job or a bad one or that they feel stressed, upset or pleased with what they have done. But they do seem to be aware that there is frequently an absence of a space to reflect, and training often seems to be significant in highlighting, and possibly rectifying, this.

The development of the concept of the reflective practitioner (Gould and Taylor 1996; Schön 1983; Schön 1987) has been important in recent years in trying to pinpoint some of the essential characteristics of professional practice, although the use of this concept is by no means clear or consistent (Eraut 1994). The concept of the reflective practitioner involves the development in the mind of a professional who is able to stand outside when acting and responding in role to the task in hand, to think about what is happening rather than just doing it. The concept has been important because it has challenged the notion of the rational and technical professional responding to complex events like a machine. Gould (1996) argues that there is considerable empirical evidence, based on research into a variety of occupations, suggesting that expertise does not derive from the application of rules or procedures applied deductively from positivist research. Instead, it is argued that practice wisdom rests upon highly developed intuition which may be difficult to articulate but can be demonstrated through practice. The concept challenges and refines the whole notion of positivist professional activity. 'Professional "problems" are not ontologically pre-defined, but have to be constructed through engagement by the practitioner with the "indeterminate zone of practice" which is typically characterised by uncertainty, uniqueness and value conflict' (p.2) Technical competence may be a necessary but insufficient ingredient to enable professionals to respond appropriately to the problems of everyday practice.

While these debates have been important in identifying some of the critical dimensions of professionalism, the observation method deepens our understanding of what it means to be reflective. It does so by focusing on the complex process of 'paying attention to', 'being receptive to' and 'holding in the mind of the observer' what is observed. These processes, I believe, involve a capacity in the observer of being able to reach out to, take in, make sense of and respond to that combination of physical, emotional and social events that is human affairs. It necessitates the existence of an internal mental space in the observer within which it is possible to develop a capacity to think and develop a knowledge of others and particularly of other's minds (Bion 1962, 1967).

I think many professionals would argue that the processes of paying attention to what you are doing and thinking about it are so routine that the statements I am making above have no special significance. However, the importance of the observation method is that it places the 'observer me' in the foreground and the 'me in role' in the background, a significant reversal of what professionalism normally means. It does this by explicitly forbidding the activities normally central to professional work, such as helping, assessing, decision making, planning or service delivery. In so doing, the security that comes from these activities disappears. While the space created by the absence of responsibility to act in role allows for a deeper consideration of what it means to observe as an activity in itself, it is clear that most people experience the removal of their 'me in role' with some ambivalence. To illustrate this point more directly it might be helpful to explore it from a slightly different perspective.

Intimate physical contact between adults involving the genitals is normally associated with one thing: a sexual relationship. Yet a gynaecological examination by a doctor means that there must be an assumption on the part of both doctor and patient that there is a complete suspension of any 'normal' sexual interest or feeling during the examination procedure, that there is nothing in the mind of the examining doctor apart from knowledge and skill. This is made possible through the notion of the professionalism of the doctor and the routine of the examination itself. It is the assumptions that go along with the boundaries of the role of doctor and the task of the examination that make the procedure possible. As soon as any question arises that might challenge this assumption – that the doctor might be an all too human being with a mind that indeed is capable of having personal feelings stirred up in the examination – then the process itself becomes unmanageable in terms of its purpose. If this possibility is not clearly excluded through the socially constructed definitions of role, the examination could easily become invaded by the meanings normally associated with such intimate contact. The resultant anxiety, whether the patient's or the doctor's, might then be overwhelming. The fact that we have such powerful mechanisms that keep these possibilities at bay and make such procedures reasonably routine is clearly important.

Most professional activity rests in some way or another on similar assumptions. The codes of conduct and ethical standards of the professions mean that 'professionals' can become involved in the affairs of their clients with a guarantee that they will not be exploited for personal gain or interest. The professional is a person in role and the 'me' is relevant only in so far as it is a combination of the ethical standards and values that exclude personal interest, and the knowledge and skill that define the professional's competence in relation to the task in hand. When undertaking an observation, the absence of the 'me in role' removes this guarantee as the observer is observing primarily for their own learning and development. While the boundaries of the method act as a guarantee that the observation will not exploit or harm the people being observed, the absence of any feedback or engagement with the observed within the accepted boundaries and tasks of professional relationships introduces sufficient ambiguity so that the question of whose needs are being met, and for what purpose, becomes an issue whether it is ever openly addressed or not. The 'observer me' is therefore a mind space within which all thoughts are possible, including greedy, self-seeking, exploitative thoughts, feelings, fantasies, desires and needs. These are, of course, the very possibilities that professionalism is a safeguard against. The existence of the 'observer me' is, therefore, an invitation to think about issues that are normally regarded in professional circles as unthinkable. The question that needs exploration is: what advantage is there in thinking about the unthinkable? Does it have any practical significance and if so what?

While the reflective practitioner is important and useful as a concept, the distinction between the 'me in role' and the 'observer me' considerably deepens the concept. Rooted as it is in object relations theory, the observation method involves people in learning about the fundamentals of relationships and the way relationships structure and determine meaning. Although the method has primarily focused on the relationships between babies and their carers, it also involves learning about internal relationships in the mind of babies and their adult carers. Attachment theory uses the term 'internal working models' (Bowlby 1973). The language used to describe these relationships involves both a physical relationship between, for instance, a mouth and a breast and a qualitative and emotional element to the relationship, such as love or hate, which, in turn, make the experience of feeding good or bad. However, this relationship is not just a relationship between two physically separate people – the baby and the carer – but is also a relationship in the mind of and inside the baby and in the mind of and inside the carer. The mother's breast can be experienced inside the baby just as the hungry baby can be experienced inside the carer. The carer might very clearly perceive themselves as feeding the actual baby but also be in touch with that powerful residue or memory and experience that have been their own experiences of being in a relationship where they have been satisfactorily or unsatisfactorily fed. What is being observed, therefore, is both a relationship in the external world between two separate individuals and a relationship inside the mind of the baby and in the mind of the mother.

As has been stated above, observing a baby feeding from the observer's point of view is clearly rooted in the physical fact of the connection between the mouth of the baby and the breast of the mother. What is being observed is also an emotive event, the qualitative aspects of which we might induce from the myriad of intricate physical interactions between them. The observer is faced with two problems. The first is trying to accurately construct the meaning of the feeding event as the baby and the mother are individually and together experiencing it. But such intimate interactions rarely leave observers unmoved. They are not immune to the emotionality of the event, the precise meaning of which they will experience in their own particular way depending on its meaning in their own mind. At the very least, for example, the observer is excluded from that feeding relationship. This might arouse feelings of envy or jealousy in the observer. Such feelings might then interfere with the observer's response to the event and, in turn, their understanding of it. If the observer feels envious of what is being observed, it is important that this can be set aside in order to see more accurately what there is to be seen. However, while it is clearly important that observers are able to monitor their own emotional responses in this way, it is also important that they should not be immune to the possibility that the envy they experience inside themselves originates from envy in the baby's mind or indeed the carer's.

The development of the process of acquiring knowledge about other people's minds is, therefore, a significant outcome from the observation method. That knowledge does depend, in part, on having a sense of the boundary between the content of one's own mind and the mind of the other. It does, however, also depend on the attentiveness and receptiveness in one's own mind to emotions and experiences that may well be painful and problematic because of one's own developmental history. Knowledge of others cannot be acquired without a knowledge of oneself. Knowledge of others cannot be a substitute for knowledge of oneself. Knowledge of oneself cannot be acquired without a relationship with others.

Residential Homes for Children

Residential children's homes can be thought of as consisting of physical, social and emotional spaces. These spaces are made available to children and young people who, for a variety of reasons but which often include physical and sexual abuse and neglect, have been separated, sometimes forcibly, from their parents. These children, therefore, bring the normal developmental needs of all children and young people, together with, often, unimaginable experiences which have left them damaged and vulnerable.

These spaces also include staff who have multiple responsibilities to reach out to, pay attention to and hold in their minds the children and young people they care for. Taking on such a role and engaging in relationships with children and young people demands a high level of knowledge and skill and very much emphasises the adult, professional qualities of people so employed.

The processes involved in making relationships between staff and young people are complex. The children and young people themselves will invariably have had mixed experiences of reaching out to adults, sometimes because of trauma in the early years and sometimes because of later changes in family circumstances or other difficulties. Sometimes their reaching out will have been met with indifference or neglect and sometimes it may have been responded to with hostility or violence. For children who have been sexually abused, this will have been compounded by bizarre and destructive mixtures of love and hate. Whatever particular experiences these children may have had, their capacity to know the contents of their own minds and relate to the contents of others will often be severely disrupted.

Staff themselves will bring their own experiences of the fundamental process of being reached out to, paid attention to and being held in the mind of others, particularly their own parents. They will also have a notion of what this means to them when they make relationships – and, especially, professional helping relationships with children and young people. However, while relationship building is a fundamental part of being a residential child care worker, what it actually means in practice is far less clear. For instance, staff will often say that while their role is parental, they are not substitute parents. Children often say that while they need and want parents, parents have caused them harm and indeed have often rejected them. Children will be aware that staff are being paid to care for them and they go 'off shift' and go on holiday at regular intervals. Therefore, the context within which relationships are made is difficult and has a significant impact on how children and staff reach out to and understand each other. Distrust, suspicion, defensiveness, hostility and hatred are as much the emotional currency of residential care as kindness, love, tenderness, sensitivity and warmth. Why staff are doing what they are doing – 'what is in their mind' – becomes a painful question for children and staff alike.

These issues are very similar to the kinds of anxieties raised in respect of gynaecological examinations. As was suggested above, the content of the professional's mind is rendered safe and also irrelevant by the definitions of professionalism and the routine of the procedure. They provide a structure for interpreting that event in a way that gives it meaning as a medical procedure rather than as an intimate sexual act or indeed as an assault. Within the space of a children's home, similar questions arise as to how to define the activities of staff as safe when many of their required tasks involve high levels of physical and emotional responsiveness and contact that cannot be as easily defined in procedural terms as they are in gynaecology. Indeed, it has been the case that, over a lengthy period of time, media attention has focused on the extensive and, in some cases, the organised and systematic abuse of children in a large number of different establishments in many different parts of the country (Levy and Kahan 1991). This has raised complex questions about the screening and appointment of suitable staff applying to work with children (DoH 1992) and the methods and procedures to be followed when working with children while in residence. While the outcome of these debates has often been helpful in establishing a framework to be followed in selection for instance, it has also attempted to deal with an issue of relationships by appearing to believe that it can sterilise the minds of those working in residential care as if they were gynaecologists. In my view, the key feature of a successful residential worker or residential home is the capacity to have an active mind that can think about relationships. It is a mind that can reach out to children and pay attention to them. It is not the mind of an abuser or the mind of a martyr but a mind that may need to know, pay attention to and hold on to what children have experienced in their minds.

The meanings that are attributed to the actions of the other and the content of their minds are powerful and cannot be ignored in residential care. How they are acknowledged and spoken about, given their anxiety provoking nature and the wish not to know of such things, is dependent, in my view, on the development of the capacity to develop an 'observer me'. What follows is a description of the use of the 'observer me' in the context of my role as consultant to residential child care staff groups.

Group Consultation in Residential Child Care

The three observations I want to describe are taken from two different establishments – a unit for older adolescents and a unit for children who have been sexually abused. The first unit takes its referrals from the authority that manages the establishment, the second is a unit run by a voluntary organisation with a number of similar units throughout the country. Both establishments have an excellent record for providing quality care. The context of the observation in both establishments is a staff group of, in one case, eight and in the other sixteen that meets weekly to explore any issues that are of concern to staff. This may include matters related to individual children or to staff. The decision as to what to bring is the responsibility of the staff members themselves and not of myself or the managers of the units.

Both of these groups face issues that are similar to those described above in relation to residential child care practice. First, what is the purpose of the group and what structures its activities? Second, what is my role as consultant to the groups?

It is a common part of most professionals' experience to meet together to discuss issues of common concern, whether this is in conferences or various training, consultative or support groups. Professionals maintain themselves through the constant development of their values, knowledge and skill base. These are the acceptable and routine topics of professional discussion. Therefore, in a group which comes together to discuss professional issues related to residential child care practice, it might be common to find topics such as child development theory, skills in working with children or knowledge about the law being the focus. It might also be common to find discussion taking place about these topics related to the circumstances of particular children in residence at the time. My role in this might be to introduce the theory as an 'expert', help the group apply it to the individual child or facilitate discussion to develop the perspectives of group members on the finer details. This, I am sure, is an accepted and acceptable view for both professionals and the public of what it means to be professional and engaged in developing an appropriate skills, knowledge and value base. It is a powerful image of professional social work training and practice – a well blended combination of appropriate values, knowledge and skills creating competent professionals who are consistent, comfortable and in control (Morrison 1994).

The processes of relationship building identified above – reaching out to, paying attention to and holding in the mind of – are topics that, on the face of it, could be part of any similar professional discussion. However, in residential child care, staff are faced with making relationships within a context where there is often a severely damaged capacity to relate – in particular, where the emotional content of these relationships contains powerfully disturbing feelings. When these are spoken about, something of the disturbing quality may be abated. When they are not, they may come to infect relationships in a damaging and, sometimes, fatal way.

The problem is how to become aware of what it is that is in the minds of children, or what children have put into the minds of staff, when some of this may be thoughts that are disturbing and anxiety provoking and cannot be thought about or spoken about.

The problem that I am faced with is similar to the staff in relation to the children. Although my role as consultant in these groups and establishments is specialised in that it doesn't require me to engage in the routine, although highly complex, activities commonly associated with the role of residential child care worker, it does face me with significant questions about the nature of my 'helping' or facilitating role. Questions such as 'What is being talked about here?', 'What might be helpful?', 'Do I know enough?', 'What is being expected of me?' and 'What do I need to do?' frequently occur. The desire and struggle to perform my role responsibly and professionally, to be helpful, to be seen as helpful and justify the time, money and effort that is being put into the groups is as significant for me as it is for any social work professional in role whatever their specific responsibilities. The emphasis of these thoughts is very much on the 'adult professional me' performing in role. However, any undue preoccupation with this side of my role could easily de-sensitise me to the rumbling anxieties identified above. The issues might then be in response to any problem in the group; 'how do I perform better in role?' rather than 'how do I pay attention to what is being felt here even if it feels unbearable to think about it?' It is the unbearable or unthinkable aspect of experience that is likely, in the longer run, to indicate what needs to be spoken about and what might indicate to the children that their deeper anxieties have been understood. The problem with attending to the group in this way is that it puts me in touch with the more primitive states of mind that are not normally considered to be a part of professional discourse. While this may not be a matter that would ever be relevant for the group to directly know about, it is a matter that is the source of my understanding about the group's relationship with the children. It is the reflective or observer part of me at work.

Both these groups, therefore, are different to a traditional model of professional education. There is no formal instruction or presentation, no reading or theory. My role in both groups is to convene the groups, attend to what is being said and to try to make sense of and explore its possible meaning. In my view, the group is concerned with constructing meaning out of experience, not of determining meaning prior to experience. This is, of course, my view and is not necessarily shared by other group members.

I am very aware in reading the accounts that follow that it sounds worryingly introspective and pretentious. I wanted to convey something of the interaction not only between myself and the group but of the internal dialogue and relationships inside of myself. If my style in reporting this stirs you up in the same way it has myself, I hope you can engage in an internal dialogue with yourself as to what this might mean for you.

(In the three accounts that follow I have tried to separate out my 'me in role' thoughts, which are printed in roman type, and actions from the 'observer me', which are printed in italics. I am aware that on the written page it is very difficult to capture accurately this distinction without distortion. To preserve confidentiality, I have changed the material so that individuals and the units themselves are not identifiable. This does raise questions of accuracy but I am aware that similar themes and discussions have taken place in a number of different groups where I have acted as consultant. I feel confident that what I am reporting has a general validity and would be recognisable in a number of settings.)

Observation 1

The group started with an uneasy silence. There were some brief comments about feeling 'tired' or 'alright' but there was no response to this and silence descended on the group once again. I asked if anybody had issues they wanted to discuss today but again there was silence.

I am aware that I am feeling despairing, cross and a bit paranoid. I know how much stress the staff are under and how much is demanded of them. There must be so many things they could talk about and that they might feel supported if they did so. I feel cross that they make the group such hard work and paranoid that the silence is something to do with me – they don't like me and hate the way I am running the group. I do wonder if they really have the capacity to use a more reflective style of learning rather than something that is more structured or provides them with more input.

In the previous group there had been some discussion about a change in the relationship between staff. They had worked hard at trying to improve their feedback to one another while on shift and this had resulted in people feeling that there was generally a better atmosphere because people were a bit more open with one another. If they were finding things difficult, they were able to say so and get help with it. If they were pleased with something else somebody had done, they said so. What I found difficult to understand was that while there was a positive feeling about how helpful it was when people talked to one another last week, nothing seemed to have been brought forward into the group this week. After the silence had lasted a few minutes, I said this.

My comments were made with some trepidation as I anticipated that they would be greeted with silence and that I was being unhelpfully critical. They didn't need to know that I thought they had failed again.

I was asked with some puzzlement what I meant. I was puzzled as to why I needed to say it again, but I did.

I then regretted this. Instead of responding to this request, I should have asked if anybody else in the group had difficulty in understanding what I meant but I so much wanted to be seen as helpful and not obstructive that I hadn't allowed myself the space to think this through. I felt I acted without thinking in an attempt to stop anybody thinking I was being depriving or awkward.

Somebody else responded by saying that the reason they didn't say anything was because they hated saying something and not getting a response from anybody. Somebody else said that they hated sitting around in a circle, it was too formal. If they had anything to say, they would prefer to say it face-to-face.

These comments were reinforcing my fear that people found the group too difficult to use constructively. I could see myself being evicted from the group in the very near future. I felt there was a significant struggle for me to survive in this group and for the group to survive in this form. Maybe it wasn't what they needed or were ready for, or maybe somebody else could do it much better.

At the same time that I was struggling with these thoughts, I was also trying to make sense of them. I think of it as trying to establish a relationship inside myself between the 'child me' full of very powerful anxieties about survival, rejection and abandonment and the 'adult/professional me' listening to that child without falsely reassuring it that everything is going to be alright or that it is being silly and should just grow up. In order to do this I need to pay attention to or observe the anxieties I was experiencing.

I was aware of the process of talking to myself in this kind of way, and also of establishing another dialogue between myself as adult/professional and supervisor trying to make sense of what these feelings might tell me about the group. This is what I think of as internal supervision. Through this process I began to see that my struggle with survival, rejection and abandonment was probably reflecting the group's struggle with these themes. In turn I imagined that the staff group's struggle reflected the children's struggle with these issues. I also thought that it would not at this point be helpful to say this. 'Why not?' I said to myself, 'Why do you want to deprive them of something they need to help relieve them of their anxieties?' 'Because they are not sufficiently hungry', I said. 'If they are not really hungry they will just play with their food and I'll end up throwing it all away.' 'Then maybe it's right to wait a bit.'

Somebody else then said that the problem with talking in the group was, for him, a bit different. A few weeks earlier he had said that he didn't know how much more he could stand. He was feeling under too much pressure. At that point he had started to cry. The group had responded to this direct show of emotion with shock. This was a senior person who was thought of as caring and very competent. Nobody had ever thought of him as being so near to breaking point. He went on to say that while in one sense he was pleased that he had shared this with the group, he had been aware that for a number of days after he had felt very self-conscious. Were people laughing at him, were people worried that he was going to collapse, did people question the decisions that he was making because he was stressed? He thought he had undermined his authority by what had happened and had been left feeling humiliated and exposed.

I said that this was a very real conflict for anybody working in residential care. We knew it was a very stressful job that often stirred up very raw emotion. Yet the culture of work and the assumptions that went along with being in a professional role seemed to demand that in order to function well, we had to keep that emotion hidden. It had no useful purpose to serve, it just interfered with the efficient performance of one's duties. If one revealed another side of oneself, the hurt and the anxiety, it raised a question as whether one was a fit person to continue in a professional role.

I felt moved by this. Here was somebody struggling with some of the issues I had been worried about. In my comments to the group I could have been talking about the staff member and I could have been talking about myself.

My comments were met with silence.

I felt I had got it wrong again and was very disappointed and angry. Why couldn't they respond to me, if only it was to tell me I had got it all wrong? The silence felt cruel. I thought I had made a breakthrough in validating the existence of a 'feeling me' within the 'me in role'. The relief of having somebody to identify with and the satisfaction of being able to make a link were very strong but I felt that I was too self-satisfied with it. Here was I, once again, trying to prove just how clever I can be. My comments weren't the magic wand that changed painful experiences into painless ones and, in turn, guarantee that I would survive in the group. Without that magic wand I was still at risk.

Looking at this from the perspective of the adult me, I was aware of just how punishing I was being to myself. After doing some work in trying to give some meaning to the group's experience up to that point, I felt the need for some recognition of this and was failing to get it. I felt angry with the group for depriving me of something that I needed and angry for putting myself in a position of needing it. I was aware that I was now pulling myself and my work to pieces. My comments may not have been perfect but might have been good enough.

Reflecting on this, I felt there was a central theme — having a go at providing something to help, feeling that it wasn't enough, acute disappointment because of this and an attack on my efforts which made them worthless. I was still feeling very anxious about the survival of the group and my survival within it. The problem with wanting to survive is that it exposed my neediness and my vulnerability and I was using my professional skills and knowledge appropriately at one level but anxiously at another to try to secure it. If the group valued my comments and saw me as a needed person, I would survive. If they didn't, I wouldn't.

Comment

While, as a human being, I can identify these primitive anxieties as my own, I felt that, in this context, they were probably related to the primitive anxieties in the group. Here were a group of competent professionals feeling overwhelmed by their experiences of trying to relate to a group of very needy young people. It terms of what I knew about the young people they were caring for, it would be difficult to know what more the staff group could be doing. Yet they felt that nothing they did was really ever good enough, no matter how hard they tried. The young people were always disappointed and angry, and, sometimes, powerfully so. The problem for myself and for the staff group was how much could we bear to feel that nothing we provided might ever be good enough, and, if it wasn't, would we survive. The young people couldn't establish a satisfactory relationship with the staff and the staff couldn't establish one with me, and my response was to try ever harder to force something professionally useful into them.

Struggling to understand these issues arises directly out of the primary task of the organisation. The primary task might be defined as providing a recuperative, caring or therapeutic environment for children and young people through relationships with them where this has not been possible in a primary or substitute family setting. However, relationship making with these young people is likely to be painful and involve facing significant distrust, avoidance, ambivalence and disappointment, however 'good enough' staff try to be. This struggle to survive in 'good enough' relationships infused with powerful anxieties can be defended against by either a persecuting quest for perfection or a hopeless despair about ever providing something that is meaningful or lasting. Both of these states act as a form of defence that is accompanied by a pervasive and unidentified anxiety that something unexpected will erupt. There will be some devastating criticism about something one has forgotten or ignored or misjudged and this is often located in routine tasks that haven't been finished.

What is difficult to recognise is the location of these feelings in what has actually been lost for the children and young people themselves – the relationships and opportunities of childhood that cannot be replaced. This recognition involves making an emotional connection with the reality that, despite one's best endeavours to relate and survive, the process of relating will never be 'good enough' because it takes place in a context of real deprivation. Relating and relationships for these children have been spoilt in a manner which is often unthinkable. The work for the children, the staff and the group is to know in what way one can survive such thoughts in a way that is meaningful without being overwhelmed by an unrecoverable depression.

Observation 2

The next example also traces this theme of the interaction between myself, the group and the task of the establishment. The issues are about the complexities of thinking about what is inside and outside when one of the contexts that define residential care is abuse.

The group opened with a question about the staff's response to recent media headlines saying that children's homes are run by abusers. Although the question was powerfully put, there was little initial response to it. One group member said that she didn't take it very seriously. She knew she wasn't an abuser and she was sure there was no abuse in the home so she just had to forget about it and get on with the job. After this dismissive statement, there was a period of silence.

I felt relieved at one level. These reports, although very worrying where they did identify extensive abuse in children's homes, did make it very hard to concentrate on the good work that was going on in other homes such as this one. It was extremely difficult to keep one's mind on the task in hand if one were continually preoccupied with whether other people thought you were abusing children or you were thinking about whether other people were abusing children. However, I did not feel comfortable with this dismissive response.

The silence was broken when a group member said very forcibly that she was feeling angry at the way she was being treated by other staff members. She felt people were ignoring her when she arrived on shift and during the shift, leaving her to do all the dirty jobs and generally exploiting her good will. She was asked if she felt it was everybody who were treating her in this way. 'No', she said, 'It wasn't, and they knew who they were'. At this point she started to cry and left the room. I asked if somebody wanted to go and see that she was alright, which somebody did.

There was a brief shocked silence. Somebody else reported that another staff member was leaving because she also felt badly treated.

I could now see why the issue of the media's identification of abuse in children's homes was so difficult to discuss – it wasn't the children who felt abused but the staff by each other. It was clearly important that this issue could be raised in the group. I felt, however, that there was a very difficult question to be faced about identifying who the abuser(s) might be, particularly in a group.

The person who had left the room returned looking distressed. Somebody asked her if she had talked to the person(s) who she felt had treated her badly. She said that she hadn't because she knew they were wrong and she didn't want to get a reputation that she was moaning and complaining and 'couldn't hack it'. Somebody else said that it was never safe to take these issues up because there were always repercussions. One of the group members who has supervisory responsibility said that when these issues were raised in supervision, the individual was encouraged to talk directly to the person concerned. However, she found it difficult to address these issues in the group because of confidentiality.

The atmosphere in the group felt persecutory and stuck. The group, it seemed, had abusers in its midst. Who were they and where were they? It seemed that if we could root them out, we could then deal with them. Although in one sense the circumstances were very different, the powerful media message of rooting out abusers and prosecuting them and imprisoning them was dominating the group. But, I thought, am I being blind to what is being said here? Are these circumstances actually different? After all, many of the circumstances discussed in the media are of incidents being reported by residents or other staff that were just not treated seriously by management in the homes or by the managers of social services departments or other bodies like the police. I may not want to think that the circumstances are similar but maybe they are.

I started to feel rather overwhelmed by all these possibilities and how to sort them out. What should I be doing, what was I responsible for?

I could see myself becoming quite panicked. However, what I felt myself most unable to do was to think. I was feeling a lot and thinking I should be doing something but I wasn't actually thinking in order to try to understand the processes at work. What seemed necessary in order to think was a coming together of the abuser with the abused in order for there to be a discussion. Questions needed to be asked about what had happened that left somebody feeling like this. Was there a misunderstanding, had the person identified as the abuser actually felt upset or dissatisfied with the work of the abused and responded in an unduly harsh manner? The fear seemed to be, however, that it wouldn't be so much a discussion as a series of accusations resulting in blame and painful recriminations that would leave people feeling exposed, vulnerable and humiliated.

Comment

The issues identified above centre on the problem of thinking when it becomes dominated by splitting (Klein 1946). The issues identified in the first topic introduced into the group and then, subsequently, in the second were too fraught by anxiety for group members to feel that there was any space that was safe enough to explore their meaning. Abuse and abusers had to be kept either outside the group or, if they were inside of it, kept hidden where they then exerted a damaging and malignant influence. Power and the abuse of power in this context was an unthinkable issue. Until a space could be made available where thinking and discussing were possible without a fear of being overwhelmed by anxiety, the experience of abuse would remain a potent force. The primary space where this work needed to take place was inside myself. Clearly, I was struggling with a number of fears of what it might mean or look like or indeed how it might be interpreted if I tried to put the issues into words. If I remained preoccupied with this and continued to hide behind the professional facade of being a consultant – that the abuse issues were outside of me – it was unlikely I would find the emotional resources to put the anxieties into words.

A similar theme arises in a different context in the next observation.

Observation 3

A group member reported that he felt very uncomfortable that a particular child had tried to cuddle him in the bedroom. This broke the home's guidelines that only limited physical contact between staff and children was permissible and it had to take place in public areas of the building. The staff member said that he hoped that nobody saw what was happening between himself and the child before he could get the child into a more public place. A rather tense discussion then took place about the problem of showing physical affection to children. Staff were professional and shouldn't get too involved with children. If you did, you had to follow the guidelines.

I felt in considerable conflict listening to this discussion. The problem of physical contact between staff as professional carers and young people is extremely difficult to handle, especially when the young people themselves have experienced sexual abuse. Children have been exploited and abused by care staff in a significant number of homes, as recent inquiries and scandals have demonstrated. It is also the case that when feeling powerless, an accusation by a child against a staff member that he or she has used the child can have damaging and serious consequences for that staff member. Protecting children and staff from such risk is clearly important and most homes have strict guidelines about what is safe and permissible.

Yet the situation being described here is ludicrous. What does physical affection mean if you are not allowed to feel anything, particularly if you are a member of staff? And what if someone sees you responding to the physical affection of a child? You must make sure that they don't think that you might actually feel something too. What do children learn from such defensive and secretive behaviour? Is there something wrong with them that makes adults behave and think in such ways? If physical affection is potentially abusive to children, isn't a form of relationship that makes it permissible only in its most sterile form equally so?

While I was debating this with myself, I became aware that in the context of the group, I was engaging in a similar process. I felt that I couldn't talk to the group about how much in conflict I felt about these things for fear of seeming to encourage them into physical relationships with children. What if they misunderstood what I was saying? What if there was a paedophile in the group? 'But John Simmonds said this was OK'. And what might they be thinking of me? Was I an abuser seeking to recruit into my inner circle? The possibilities seemed horrendous and I felt I wanted to protect myself from planting anything suspicious in people's minds. I wasn't going to do anything that put me at risk.

But here I was in the role of consultant and, presumably, sorted on these issues. I was supposed to be helping them to think about what was being said, but, in fact, I was feeling as stuck in my own mind as they were. It became clearer to me that this dilemma was what needed to be put into words.

I said that I thought that the person who had brought this issue to the group showed some courage and was taking some risk. The possibility of being misunderstood, particularly for a man working in residential care, was very real. However, turning away from the spontaneous show of affection from a child seemed cruel and rejecting. If there was one thing staff might give children, it was something of the warmth and friendship that they had missed out on in a safe way in their own families. However, the fact was that both things were true at the same time. It could be both unsafe and it could be felt to be rejecting. This was the painful reality of life in a residential home for children and, while one might wish that it was otherwise, it would be a deception to pretend that it was so.

I felt terrible in saying this. I wanted to find a way of saying that it was not only important but necessary to show spontaneous affection to children and it was safe to do so if you did x,y or z as a precaution. Unfortunately, there was no simple or responsible way of constructing such a desired outcome.

The group responded with a depressed silence.

Comment

Both the image and reality of children in children's homes naturally evokes a powerful desire to surround them with warmth and affection. This feeling pervades both the staff group and myself in this observation. Yet within this specific event, there are a complex set of issues. These centre around the difference between something which appears to be nothing more than a spontaneous hug and a responsibility to think about the nature of relationships in a context where children have experienced abusive adults who have no idea of the difference between children's needs and their own. However, this responsibility, while recognisably important, brings its own dilemmas because to think in this way is painful. First, it highlights the fact that these children are in residential care and not with their families and this reality is, in the truest sense, a depressing thought. Second, it faces staff with recognising that their role has a 'therapeutic' element to it that requires them to move beyond the obvious, easy and unthinking. Third, making relationships is a difficult thing to do in a meaningful sense and sometimes that means delaying gratification of what in other circumstances may be the most caring and human response. The question then is what is the value of relationships that are rooted in this kind of thinking? If they are not 'ideal' replacements for what has been lost in the child's family of origin, what value do they have? If we are to avoid an abusive recreation of what has been, is there any value in the procedure-led professionalism that is meant to be their safeguard?

Concluding Thoughts

Further exploration of these questions is beyond the scope of this chapter. However, what I hope they do demonstrate is that by attending to thoughts which are almost unbearable, it starts to open up the territory of learning about relationships that are neither an abuse of the power of adult carers nor a sterile pretence of them. For this to happen, it means paying attention to that jumble of emotions that lay beyond what is usually considered to be adult or, more particularly, professional thinking. It means thinking about thoughts which do not conform to the image of the professional – consistent, comfortable and in control. It also moves beyond the image of the reflective practitioner as an easy option to the mechanical routines of 'modern' competency-based ideology. But it does open up the possibility of making connections with the raw material of the human mind and of establishing a link with the experience of others who have experienced oppression, discrimination and poverty of opportunity.

References

Bick, E. (1964) 'Notes on infant observation in psychoanalytic training.' *International Journal of Psychoanalysis 45*, 558–566.

Bion, W. (1962) *Learning from Experience*. London: Heinemann.

Bion, W. (1967) *A Theory of Thinking in Second Thoughts*. London: Heinemann.

Bowlby, J. (1973) *Attachment and Loss, Vol. 2 Separation*. London: Hogarth Press.

Brafman, A. (1988) 'Infant observation.' *International Review of Psychoanalysis 15*, 45–61.

DoH (1992) *The Report of the Committee of Inquiry into the Selection Development and Management of Staff in Children's Homes*. London: HMSO.

Eraut, M. (1994) *Developing Professional Knowledge and Competence*. London: Falmer Press.

Gould, N. (1996) 'Introduction: social work education and the "crisis of the professions".' In N. Gould and I. Taylor (eds) *Reflective Learning for Social Work*. Aldershot: Arena.

Gould, N. and Taylor, I. (eds) (1996) *Reflective Learning for Social Work*. Aldershot: Arena.

Klein, M. (1946) 'Notes on some Schizoid Mechanisms' in *Envy and Gratitude and Other Works. The Writings of Melanie Klein, Vol. 3*. London: Hogarth Press.

Levy, A. and Kahan, B. (1991) *The Pindown Experience and the Protection of Children*. Staffordshire County Council.

Miller, L., Rustin, M., Rustin, M. and Shuttleworth, J. (1989) *Closely Observed Infants*. London: Duckworth.

Morrison, T. (1994) *Staff Supervision in Social Care: An Action Learning Approach*. Harlow: Longmans.

Pietroni, M. (ed) (1991) *Right or Privilege? Postqualifying Training for Social Workers with Special Reference to Child Care, CCETSW Study 10*. London: CCETSW.

Schön, D.A. (1983) *The Reflective Practitioner. How Professionals Think in Action*. New York: Basic Books.

Schön, D.A. (1987) *Educating the Reflective Practitioner: Towards a New Design for Teaching and Learning in the Professions*. San Francisco: Jossey Bass.

Trowell, J. (1991) 'Use of observational skills in social work training.' In M. Pietroni (ed) *Right or Privilege? Postqualifying Training for Social Workers with Special Reference to Child Care, CCETSW Study 10*. London: CCETSW.

Trowell, J. and Miles, G. (1991) 'The contribution of observation training to professional development in social work.' *Journal of Social Work Practice 5*, 1, 51–60.

CHAPTER FIVE

Beyond the Bureauprofessional

Observational Study as a Vehicle for Interprofessional Learning and User-centred Practice in Community Care

Marilyn Miller-Pietroni

Introduction: The Bureauprofessional

George had a severe stroke at the age of 85 which left him confused and clumsy and unable to go to the lavatory on his own. It was agreed that he and his wife, who was also disabled, would go and live with their daughter in her basement flat. Since the hospital was wanting to discharge George, their occupational therapist (OT) exceptionally did a home visit to assess what adaptations and aids would be necessary. Both daughter and hospital occupational therapist contacted the local social services department to alert them of the urgency and to provide this information 'up front'.

The social worker, however, told the hospital OT that there would be a wait of at least one month and possibly more before an assessment could be made. The hospital OT's assessment 'would not be acceptable to the local authority', she explained, because 'their criteria are different'.

The social worker did not visit the client or his daughter but telephoned to explain the position of the 'bureau'.

The assessment visit was made two months later. The daughter had by then paid for some of the aids and adaptations recommended by the hospital OT. She was, however, further upset because the condition of her father had deteriorated and her mother was very distressed. Three people came to the assessment visit: the Care Manager, a trainee OT and the senior OT. They carried out a full assessment, including an assisted 'walk upstairs'.

The daughter felt overwhelmed but merely said, 'No wonder there is a waiting list...'

The next day George died.

Two weeks later, the daughter received a letter stating what financial and other help the local authority could provide. She did not reply. The letter was not followed up by the local authority.

The context in which social work is practised is usually bureaucratic: a social services department, a hospital or clinic, or a voluntary organisation. As 'bureauprofessionals', social workers have to work within these organisational frameworks and are accountable to them.

There is, and always has been, an intrinsic conflict between the complexity of social work assessments that have to be made in practice and the lumbering organisational procedures through which professional and statutory authority is managed and scarce resources are allocated. Decision-making structures within the 'bureau' are usually established by local policy guidelines which seek to standardise practice on the one hand, whilst rationing scarce resources (according to agreed criteria) on the other. These guidelines can be exercised in a defensive way that is insensitive to the human aspects of the life crises and chronic situations which present to social services. Mostly, such guidelines are not understood by service users and will *only* be experienced by them at the human level. As a result, the assessments which mark the access point to services often seem to be and are, in fact, complex, obscure and long-winded.

The bureaucratised nature of response to need in social services stands in sharp contrast to the culture of assessment in general practice, which can be summarised as: 'six minutes for the patient', same-day home visits for emergency or prioritised cases and a culture of individualised responsibility and decision making (Balint and Norrell 1973). At its worst, the general practice system is idiosyncratic and high-handed, at its best it is swift and has an admirable quality of economically delivered one-to-one precision from which social work could do well to learn. To the service user, who may well be receiving services from health and social care systems at the same time, as in the example above, the contrast in response times and professional cultures can, in practice, be both striking and baffling.

Part of the reason for these professional differences lies in the nature of basic professional training and the core professional identity to which it gives rise. GPs, though now part of a managed, primary care-led NHS, have been trained intensively and at length into an individual decision making culture. Their training pays due attention, through carefully planned rotations, to both generalist and specialist knowledge and experience so that all-round confidence is established. They learn to stand alone (Spratley and Pietroni 1992).

Social workers, on the other hand, tend to be undertrained both generically and in specialist areas. Not surprisingly, their professional culture gives prominence to collaborative thinking and decision making within the context of the social work team. Furthermore, the hierarchical decision making structure of the local authority – employer of the majority of social workers – allows little room for discretionary action. The basic professional training – the Diploma in Social Work – is short (two years), overloaded and under-resourced. However skilfully it is delivered, it cannot provide an adequate foundation for the complexity of social work assessment and practice that follows qualification. Furthermore, high-quality supervised practice placements are scarce and under-funded, so many social workers enter the field ill-equipped for the serious and complex responsibilities that follow qualification and few will have subsequent access to regular high-quality supervision.

That social workers are expected to develop in conditions of such educational poverty inevitably shapes their professional culture and self-esteem. Front-line social workers have little influence over policy or the resource framework of their practice or associated guidelines. These factors further reinforce a sense of being cogs in a large machine in which limited, prescribed responses are what is expected and required. For example, in the recently publicised child protection inquiry in Cambridgeshire, front-line staff were severely criticised for failing to appreciate the risks which ultimately led to the death of Ricky Neave (Bridge Consultancy 1997). Yet staff in that team had several times alerted management to the dangers of understaffing and lack of supervision. Their warnings were either unheard or ignored.

This chapter explores how observational learning can help to address some of these conflicts between social work policy, theory and practice by reducing defensive bureauprofessional behaviour and generating enough inner space in the individual worker to restore human and creative responses to need. The chapter will begin with a brief review of two aspects of the policy context of health and social care which deeply affect how social work is practised and will go on to describe a multiprofessional Masters programme in which observational study is a key feature. The chapter concludes with a theoretical analysis of the social defences in social work and a discussion of the impact on those social defences of observational learning.

The Policy Context: Two Cross-Currents

There is not space within the constraints of this chapter to carry out a significant policy analysis. However, one of the hazards of observational study is that in freeing professionals from the mindset of the bureau-professional and concentrating more on the emotional impact of individual experience, the statutory context may not be sufficiently addressed.

A brief comment on two currents in recent policy change follows because it is considered relevant to the reflective 'inner work' that needs to be undertaken as a result of observational learning. Indeed, this chapter will argue that 'field' or 'agency' observation of a health or social care organisation as a system at work can and should be undertaken and that it is educationally as important as the observation of interacting individuals. It is suggested that by achieving a reflective and critical distance from both the content and context of practice, observational study is able to perform a more profound 'circuit-breaking' function that counters the pressure toward dehumanising bureauprofessional behaviour which has been exacerbated by the policy changes.

First Policy Current: The Bureauprofessional in a Supermarket of Care

Most professional social workers (and their close colleagues in health) have found that basic professional values, particularly altruism, have been challenged by the 'market' approach to care introduced in the 1990s. The market of care was established by organisationally separating the purchase and provision of services (the 'purchaser–provider split'). Each 'episode' or individual 'package' of care (such as the assessment and number of home adaptations in the example described above) must now be quantified and costed.

The resulting packages of care are aggregated into service provision contracts which are bought by purchasing units and monitored for their performance over specified periods of time. Policy decisions about provision are made at policy and management level according to centrally agreed resource limits and service rationing criteria. Additionally, service commissioning units review the increasingly accurate profiles of need in a community against the cost and performance of existing provider contracts and seek to fine-tune the system by commissioning services where need is falling between the gaps or cheaper routes can be found.

This market approach to care was introduced by the Conservative government following a major report more commonly known as 'The Griffiths Report' (1989) written by Sir Roy Griffiths and drawing heavily on his previous experience as chairman of a leading supermarket. The resulting legislation, *The National Health Service and Community Care Act 1990* (DoH 1990), sought to ensure that public services were managed through an 'internal market' system which was expected to reduce costs, improve efficiency and provide better opportunities to monitor quality.

These major changes brought in two new languages, previously alien to the professional health or social care worker: the language of the market and the language of large-scale business management. In fact, the change in professional language was so great that it became necessary to publish glossaries to help professionals understand and adapt. But whilst new languages (and with them the values of the supermarket) were being introduced, old ones, more closely linked to small-scale individualised service, were put at risk.

A phrase of great significance in this language debate was 'unmet need' because it sat on the boundary of old and new languages. An offspring of the new terminological set of 'needs assessment', 'care management' and 'care packages', this phrase also sat quite comfortably in the earlier language set of social work practice which conveyed the values of professional altruism more explicitly. When needs assessment was first introduced, each individual set of needs assessment and care management forms charted the 'unmet need' for a particular client. When it was discovered that such recording would render social services departments legally liable for any mishaps resulting from that unmet need, departments were instructed by the Department of Health to collect such data in an aggregated way only (i.e. not on individualised care management forms). Subsequently, when it became clear that budgets were not going to be available for meeting many such needs, the experience of many social workers was that a subtle bureaucratic 'erasure' took place.

The bureauprofessional working within agency guidelines must adhere to such changing policy edicts and their ensuing bureauprofessional practices, but the cost in terms of stress and compromised professional values is dear. What observational study does is to help prevent that stress from generating a professional 'second skin' of the defensive kind illustrated by the example above and described by Bick (1968) in her now classic paper on the use of observational study.

Second Policy Current: 'We are all Equal Here'

At the same time as introducing the terminology and values of the market, the 1990 Act introduced a 'user-centred' philosophy. Consumerist in conception (in line with the supermarket culture of which it was a part), this new policy sound-bite conveniently appeared to build on the forces toward democratisation of public services which had been taking place somewhat slowly over the preceding decade.

This democratisation of services had been signalled earlier in health care by the introduction of community health councils and in social care by the 'partnership' philosophy introduced by *The Mental Health Act 1983* (DoH 1983) and later popularised following *The Children Act 1989*. It was appealing because it signalled an end to the elitist excesses of prof-essionalism. It was seductive because it implied that a new and more committed form of egalitarianism was at work in which the patronising distance of old-style professionalism would be replaced by a new connectedness with the needs of service-users.

This new and explicit focus on the user also appeared to indicate that large-scale bureaucracies would develop a capacity for which they were not previously known: the capacity for listening. Press releases from the Department of Health began to use seductive phrases like 'user-centred seamless service'. However, resources were erratically distributed and the pace of reorganisation (and renaming) was such that the gap between rhetoric and reality was widened. Increasingly defensive 'organisational routines' and practices of the kind described by Argyris and Schön (1974) were, therefore, inevitable. These organisational routines increased the pressure on individual professionals to develop that 'second skin' in order to survive the pain of watching professional values eroded by market pressures and the 'newspeak'.

Backed up by a range of charters, inspection units and complaints systems (for example, *The Patient's Charter* (DoH 1991)), the new language of the user-centred approach was able to draw together a number of previous interest groups from both left and right of the ideological spectrum. Thus the controversial new legislation enjoyed a smoother start than might otherwise have been predicted.

Caught in the Cross-Currents

Professionals inevitably became caught in these cross-currents. On the one hand the democratising partnership and consumer-oriented philosophies appeared to encourage them to draw closer to the world of the user and, on the other, professional distance and anaesthesia were fostered by cost-led, centrally managed, bureaucratised care systems accompanied by a flood of departmental guidelines, evidence-based criteria, audit cycles and service protocols.

Such cross-currents are confusing and make it difficult to think. Some would say they induce a state of professional shock. Thus the altruism and humanity which are part of the core personal identity of social workers are put at risk. It is hardly surprising that in such conditions individually-tailored care sometimes gave way to the 'ready-made' response of the bureau-professional.

At the University of Westminster we have found that observational study of individual service users helps professionals to get inside the experience of the client or patient in a more genuinely user-centred way. Observation of a small system at work also helps the policy and organisational systems to be seen for what they are: an invitation to 'bureau-think' and 'bureau-talk'.

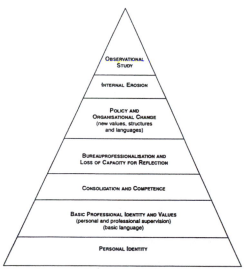

Figure 5.1: The layers of personal, professional and bureauprofessional identity

Together, they help the professional to break free from the impoverished mental circuit of the bureauprofessional and to concentrate on the needs of individuals and their inevitable fate at the hands of large systems at work (See Figure 5.1).

The following section describes how a reliable challenge to bureauprofessional identity can be offered by observational study when used as a tool of a reflective practice approach (Schön 1992).

Reflective Practice and Observational Study: Challenging the Bureauprofessional Tendency

The reflective practitioner, according to Schön (1983, 1987), may be defined as one who recognises the intrinsic limits of professional knowledge and action and builds in a cycle of rigorous reflection that maximises the capacity for critical thought and stimulates creativity and intuition. This approach, Schön suggests, produces a sense of 'professional artistry', greater freedom of thought and a connection with, rather than distance from, clients. This close connection is hard to sustain in the face of repeated human suffering.

At the University of Westminster observational study is considered the core learning experience for developing a reflective practice approach (see below: The Observational Study Module). There follow two examples of the observation and reflection process in action. The first individual observation was carried out by a recent social work student. The student describes an example of elder care in a Community Hospital. The student carried out ten weekly, one-hour observations of a 93-year-old man in a long-term placement. The second agency observation was carried out by a GP at a local social services reception area.

The first observation demonstrates the process of 'banalisation' (Hadjiiski 1987) at work in the hospital ward. 'Banalisation' as a concept is addressed further in the discussion below. It can here be defined as the mental numbness or 'second skin' that the bureauprofessional is forced to develop as a result of the context and content of their work.

The professionals observed by this social worker happen to be nurses, but the other core professions (general practice and social work), when observed, demonstrate the same features. The example shows how observational study can deconstruct the process of bureauprofessionalisation for a mature student, generating subtle and precise reflections.

As I entered the ward, I noticed that all office doors were closed. At the far end a group of nurses were crowding round a patient trying to decide the best way to put a pillow behind her head. One of the nurses roughly pulled the pillow out and declared that they had got it all wrong.

I was reminded of my student days on the cot and 'chair' wards of a large psychiatric hospital some fifteen years ago. Not much had changed.

Eventually, one of the nurses came and introduced me to Arthur, who was sitting with his daughter-in-law and wife. He was in a wheelchair with a dirty-looking sheepskin rug draped over the back and was wearing those slippers with a Velcro strap. He was also wearing a heavy track suit, which, though I understood the reasons for it, seemed suddenly ironical for a man in his nineties who had suffered two strokes. His creased shirt collar also reminded me of the clothes on that old psychiatric ward. Underneath his shirt I could make out a thermal vest, the edge of which looked hard and was covered in dried food. His right arm hung loosely by his side but I noticed his left hand was making a fist.

Between our chairs a tatty red notebook sat on a table…

He mumbled something to me.

'I'm sorry I don't understand,' I said.

'He wants to go home dear,' said the old lady…

'…now, now, boy. Don't cry. We don't need any of that.'

She smiled. I felt uncomfortable.

'He's tube-fed at night,' she told me, as if he were not there.

'…Come on, Arthur, please don't cry, boy. You know you can't go home. Now move your leg, like the doctor said.'

Arthur mumbled something, sat back in his chair, pulled his lip inwards, closed his eyes and began to cry.

'That pad is his lifeline,' said the daughter-in-law. She touched him gently and gave it to him with a pencil.

Quicker than I expected he wrote a short sentence with his good hand. She read it and showed it to me.

'Come on Arthur,' she repeated the refrain. 'You know you can't go home…'

She got up with a sigh and took the cups back to the voluntary shop.

> 'Luckily, I'm not on my own', went on the wife. Nodding in the
> direction of her daughter-in-law.
> With a visible sniff she said, 'I've got a son who lives near...' (Tho-
> mas 1995, pp.2–3)

This student was a highly experienced trainer. He might have expected a
more straightforward experience from his first observational study, but, by
giving up his usual professional role and responsibilities, he opened himself
up to witness the full force of institutionalised bureauprofessional behaviour:
the nurses huddle together and establish their pecking order whilst ignoring
his entry to the ward. He states that he expected the world to have moved on
from his own previous hospital work experience but found that it had not
changed – a deeply depressing fact.

He also had time to think anew and, in so doing, discovered the
incongruity of that ubiquitous track suit which seems to have become a kind
of practical, yet grotesque, 'baby-grow' for disabled and elderly people. He
noticed the caked food on the thermal vest and the creased shirt collar and he
heard, saw and felt Arthur's plea to go home. He found himself confronted
not only with the pain and suppressed anger of individual helplessness but
also with those embedded family dynamics that confront the practitioner at
every turn and limit the usefulness of even highly skilled interventions.

So the chronic patterns of institutional and individual life were here
opened up to detailed scrutiny, simply described and powerfully felt. It is no
one person's fault that things are as they are, but, by ensuring that
professional defences are disturbed in a productive way, the system and the
human beings within it can be re-viewed. Thus habitual patterns of
professional and institutional behaviour become available for influence.

The second 'agency observation' took place in the reception area of a
local social services office. An important aspect of this observation is that it
was carried out by a general practitioner but was reported on in a seminar in
which social workers, community nurses and voluntary sector workers were
present. Selections of the text have been made that highlight the impact of
the organisational and professional differences on the GP observer.

> This set of observations took approximately six weeks to set up.
> There has been considerable resistance and hesitancy... Today is my
> first visit... The area office concerned operates as a children and
> families unit.
> I am required to meet the area manager before I can begin. The

department incidentally, is on the ground floor of a multi-storey building at a busy junction, some way from any residential area.

I walk into a small reception area presided over by a small reception window which is locked shut. A woman opens it up and asks me who I am, I explain and she locks it shut again, and then opens it to say the area manager will be with me shortly. The window is then closed again and remains locked shut... After a short wait, the area manager arrives and makes me feel very welcome...she takes me back to the 'duty office' where I meet the staff...I am eventually positioned in a corner where I can see both the main work area and the reception window.

There is a fair amount of noise and excitement in the office and the overall atmosphere seems to be informal, relaxed and supportive... Two staff members drift through the office and move out into the reception area. A family seems to be waiting to be seen... I can hear a child playing... The two staff members move out into the reception area and proceed to have conversation that takes at least five minutes...I cannot make out the substance but know that it must be clearly audible in the duty office and the reception area. They eventually finish and both areas quieten down... Social workers leaf through reports...one goes to make coffee...another goes shopping...there is some general chat about shopping and clothes...

At this point a male social worker marches into the office. He is directive and assertive and seems to shatter the peaceful atmosphere. 'Is my client here?... Where is he...?'

Apparently the client has not turned up. He marches out again.

The telephone rings and is answered by a female social worker. There have obviously been a number of preceding conversations between the client and this social worker about the purchase of a baby buggy... The client wants an expensive version and the social worker says a good one is available at half the price at a well-known store... The client does not want that one...

The reception bell rings for the first time since my arrival...I can just make out the face of an old woman peering through the window... One of the social workers goes over and lets her in and talks to her...it transpires that she is homeless and has been sent to the wrong office...she leaves somewhat grumpily... The bell goes again... Another old woman appears who wants a list of doctors in the area...again she has been directed to the wrong place...but this time the social worker gets into conversation with the woman and discovers that she can actually advise her as they live near each other and she knows which doctors are available. The woman leaves sounding grateful...

Now the telephone rings and another social worker discusses with a client her request to have her child back home from a temporary fostering arrangement...the social worker is obviously tense dealing with the situation...and concludes by repeating twice, 'I hear what you are saying...' As I get up to leave, the social worker apologises, '...that it has been so quiet today...' (Fermie 1994, pp.1–3)

This GP brings out the difference between patterns of reception in a GP's surgery and those in a social services area office by his initial pre-occupation with the repeatedly locked window. Although violence is increasing in general practice, to have a locked window is rare. On the contrary, many general practices actively cultivate a sense of easy access to help patients feel less anxious or intimidated when visiting the doctor. In social services, the experience of the repeatedly locked window, therefore, stands starkly.

The social work hierarchy is also in evidence and he notes it by his language: 'I am *required* to meet the area manager...'. The ritual of access to the department is, in fact, marked by a series of hurdles which have to be overcome: the six weeks it took to set the observation up, the locked door and window, the first contact via 'the boss'. This access ritual experienced by the GP is mimicked by the experience of the two clients that seek access in person and find they are in the wrong place as a result of poor or lacking information. However, they are treated differently: one is sent away and one is 'helped'. Access by the telephone seems easier and the range of social work practice quickly becomes apparent, including its inherent stresses and strains.

Finally, he seems concerned at the use of the client's reception area as a place for staff conversations and implies that there may be a potential confidentiality hazard here, just as he also notes the shopping talk and the coffee. The social worker's final comment about 'not much going on today' seems also to indicate some unease on their part about the contrast between a busy general practice (with up to twenty patients per doctor per two- or two-and-a-half-hour surgery) and the pace and nature of calls at their office in this hour (three clients and two telephone calls to four social workers). This observation is important in the light of well-documented tensions between the two professions about collaboration, particularly over GP attendance at case conferences. However, these comments and observations are not necessarily about relative workloads, even if they seem that way. They may, over a period of ten weeks, emerge quite differently and be more associated with differences in task and work culture between the two professions.

Always in an agency observation there are at least three observations occurring: the one that is described, the internal 'home agency' and the associated interprofessional preconceptions. The implicit contrast and the dialectic here between the social services area office observed, the one which pre-exists in the mind and the real one that is observed is available for discussion in the multiprofessional seminar. Understanding between the professions can be enhanced in this way. Better still, the professions can learn from each other about different ways of doing things and routine organisational habits can be heightened and questioned.

Reflective Practice and Observational Learning in an Interprofessional Masters Programme

I will now describe more fully the place and significance of observational study within the MA in Primary Health and Community Care: Towards Reflective Practice (MACPHC) at the University of Westminster (UW). Students like the two above who have undertaken the programme now number more than seventy and include the full range of professions involved in providing health and social care: general practitioners, social workers, all community nursing disciplines (health visitors, district nurses, community psychiatric nurses, practice nurses and nurse practitioners), professions allied to medicine (occupational therapists, physiotherapists), housing officers and members of the voluntary and independent sector who are working above the level of individual care.

The programme was developed in 1990–1992 by a multiprofessional team working within principles established in 1989 by core staff in the Education and Training Unit of a small charity: Marylebone Centre Trust (MCT). The Trust itself was closely linked to the interprofessional and interagency approach of the Marylebone Health Centre (MHC).

The Rationale for Observational Study

The multiprofessional development team identified observational study as a vehicle for both interprofessional learning and the development of reflective practice. Their reasons were as follows:

- to exclude professional jargon
- to foster a shared language that was neither professionally-centred nor culturally-specific
- to increase the capacity for thinking about practice in depth
- to humanise practice in the interests of clients/patients/users
- to encourage a whole person approach.

In other words, observational study was unanimously identified as a vehicle for developing advanced practice.

The multiprofessional development team had within its experience a range of different methods, models and traditions of observational study:

- shadowing a colleague on a daily or weekly basis (community nursing)
- participant observation in anthropological field study (medical anthropology)
- the psychoanalytic/psychodynamic approach (Tavistock Clinic social work)
- organisational observation (Tavistock Clinic programme on institutions)
- interactive observation as used by Native American Indians in training the medicine man (GP field research)
- participant and non-participant observation as a research method (all professions).

Needless to say, the full implications of this unusually wide range of approaches to observation were not exhaustively debated. However, the original heterogeneity and the open-mindedness signalled toward observational theory and method continue to provide inspiration. The current staff team believe that observational study is a means of developing skilled and sensitive practitioners capable of thinking for themselves, collaborating across differences and, where necessary, having the evidence to argue a policy case in the face of current trends towards managerialism.

The curriculum interactions within the programme were considered carefully (see below). Individual observations take place in parallel with learning about health and social policy in the first instance. This prevents any dissociation from policy realities from taking place. The second observation of an agency or small system at work is timed to coincide with other organisational learning, including a group dynamic event known as 'Pride and Prejudice in Interprofessional Work'. A practical space for integration of learning over time is achieved by a workshop that continues throughout the year and to which examples of current practice are brought for discussion and critique by the multiprofessional student group. The second year dissertation has to include use of all year one learning, including observational study. As part of gathering data for their dissertations, some students take the opportunity to carry out further observational study in the second year. Several have taken the method back to their own agencies as a vehicle for staff and organisational development.

Year One

1. Theories, Policies and Current Issues (autumn).

2. The Reflective Practitioner 1: Observation of Practices (all year).

3. Interprofessional, Interagency and Intersector Collaboration 1: Organisational Life (spring).

4. The Reflective Practitioner 2: Individual Development (academic skills–all year).

5. Interprofessional, Interagency and Intersector Collaboration 2: Reflective Workshop (all year).

Year Two

6–8. Dissertation.

The Observational Study Module

As previously explained, observational study is viewed as the core module in the reflective practice approach because it allows time for reflection-on-action and reflection-in-action (Schön 1983, 1987) to occur week-by-week, thus establishing a reflective discipline for students that deepens over time. The module requires that students carry out two or three observational study placements over a total of twenty weeks. A module is approximately 50 hours and the programme can be taken on a day-release or modular basis.

The first placement is described as 'individual observation' and students are asked to observe an individual receiving health or social services for one hour each week for ten weeks, to write up their observations – including their own feelings and reflections after the event – and then to bring that record to a seminar for discussion. They are asked to select the individual from outside of their own agency and field of practice to increase their learning and their critical distance. Observations have included children in day nurseries, elders in day or residential care, mental health service users in day and residential care, prisoners, refugees, people with illness or disabilities living at home or in residential care.

The second set of observations are of an agency or small system at work, again observed for one hour each week but this time over ten weeks or two consecutive sets of five weeks. Again, the student is asked to look for a placement outside of their usual field of practice – in health if they work in social services and vice versa. Observations have included GP reception areas, police stations, Social Security offices, a Citizens Advice Bureau reception area, a community nursing office, a nursery class in a school, accident and emergency departments, residential homes, day centres, an HIV/Aids Unit and a religious refugee advice centre. The same agency is observed each week for one hour, which then provides a living picture of the agency at work over time. The continuity allows the student to move from habitual or snap judgements to deeper understanding. Students describe how this opens their eyes to their in-built prejudices. Their understanding of the complexities involved deepens over the ten-week period and is also transferred later to other areas of work.

The module thus aims to use observational study to establish an awareness of individual communications at sea within complex human systems of organisation and deepens an appreciation of the complexity of interprofessional and interagency collaboration.

Seminar discussions allow a range of feelings and possible interpretations to be explored; enriched, particularly, by the interprofessional composition of the seminar group. Students discover that GPs, nurses and social workers use different language, have different professional values and write differently. Their assumptions about professional stereotypes and pecking orders are challenged and, at best, they discover their common humanity and lay some of their prior prejudices.

For assessment, students submit a sample of three of their observations, including at least one from each series. They are asked to add a paragraph putting their observation into its organisational context. They must also include their subsequent reflections and are advised to avoid premature or speculative theorisations. The emphasis is on the direct emotional impact of what has been observed and producing simple observational records that convey the human aspects of what is observed or, as in the examples above, the tension between human need on the one hand and the dehumanising effects of human institutions and some aspects of human interaction on the other. The assessment is deliberately simple and atheoretical, although its claims to postgraduate status have been sometimes challenged as a result. Interestingly, there is a tension here. The learning needs of advanced professional practice include deepening the appreciation of complexity and increasing flexibility of thought and knowledge at the same time as achieving greater simplicity in language and expression. The requirements of postgraduate status include theoretical sophistication and choice. A modular programme, however, can balance this tension across the modules.

The programme described above does not offer a module on human growth and development and the observational study approach is not used as a vehicle for this area of learning as on some other programmes.

A brief account of the values that underpin the programme and were developed by the original Marylebone Centre Trust multiprofessional development team during the development phase now follows.

The Working Principles of Marylebone Centre Trust (MCT): Values at Work

The principles governing the work of the original Marylebone Centre Trust, founded in 1989, shaped the culture and values that underpinned the eventual University of Westminster programme (MCT 1991; Pietroni, M. 1992). They also helped a heterogeneous staff team to find their common foundations. They have mostly stood the test of time and are worth summarising here:

> 'Users of health and community care services need to be offered knowledge, skills and support to enable them to take an active interest in their health and emotional well-being. They can also share responsibility for helping to maintain the organisations designed to promote health and community care. Professionals therefore need to be encouraged to develop methods of work which enable them to share their own power,

Figure 5.2: Empowering the user/client/patient
Stephen Appleby for Marylebone Centre Trust, 1993

Figure 5.3: Sustaining the caregiver
Stephen Appleby for Marylebone Centre Trust, 1993

Figure 5.4: Caring in context
Stephen Appleby for Marylebone Centre Trust, 1993

knowledge and expertise with clients, at personal and organisational levels.'

'The overall health and emotional well-being of the practitioner is a vital factor in all encounters between practitioners and users. Management of the self in a range of contexts is also essential to prevent burn-out. Personal development, group support and staff supervision therefore need careful attention.'

'All health and community care, whether reliant on 'high tech' and high skill or empathic exchange, is undertaken within a social context that includes different aspects of the lives of users and carers alike. This contextual approach to health and community care means exploring personal, family, organisational and political aspects of service provision.'

Figure 5.5: Working collaboratively
Stephen Appleby for Marylebone Centre Trust, 1993

Figure 5.6: Acknowledging limitations
Stephen Appleby for Marylebone Centre Trust, 1993

'The practice of health and community care involves a number of professions and voluntary workers collaborating together. This collaboration needs to occur across disciplines, within groups, and to involve clients directly. The development of collaborative skills must therefore form an essential part of all education and training programmes.'

'The finite nature of financial resources and the slow pace of organisational cultural change are facts of life, along with the limited power and ability of professionals and other workers to bring about direct change. Similarly, some clients are able to use health and community services to more effect than others. These limitations, and their accompanying frustrations are at the heart of understanding and surviving in primary health and community care.'

Discussion

The Implications of Policy Change

If observational study is to enhance reflective practice by increasing the intuitive connections between 'the high ground of academic rigour' and the 'swamp of practice' (Schön 1983), it must be contextualised in the real world of policy, organisation and service delivery. One of the key factors which has reinforced bureauprofessional behaviour in the UK has been rapid and fundamental policy change. The working context of health and social care has changed so dramatically over the last ten years that many consider the resulting individual and organisational turmoil to be even greater than when the national health and social services were set up in the late-1940s (Leathard 1995; Pietroni, P.C.P. 1996). Many posts have been cut or renamed as a result of the policy changes and the experience of having to reapply for one's own post or finding that it has been written out of the latest reorganisation are commonplace. A working context of this kind produces frustration and major stress about job security and domestic survival, which, in turn, further constricts the quality of attention available for complex practice.

The anxiety about individual and organisational survival produced by such fundamental policy change (like any anxiety about survival) is of a very primitive or fearful kind. It inevitably reduces the resilience of the workforce overall and reinforces the individual professional's need for respite from the pressures of finding tailor-made responses to individual need. That respite can sometimes be secured by temporarily sinking into a kind of anonymity through membership of a faceless organisational large group or 'horde': the social services bureau.

This submersion of independent thought, and, with it, individualised language, into the terminological sea of the group is what Julia Kristeva describes as taking on the mindset of 'the cradle' (Oliver 1993 and discussion below). It has many of the features of Bion's (1961) well-known concept of the mental life of groups: basic assumption dependency, a state in which highly intelligent and skilled group members behave as if they were incapable of individual thought and in unconscious fantasy wait for a heroic group leader to rescue them and show them the way. Policy makers, far from providing such wished-for heroic leadership, have silently replaced social work with care-management; a term which often means managing shrinking public care commitments and a change in social values.

The pressures of such fundamental change hit both individual and system at an emotionally deep level whilst throwing codes of language and practice into the air and replacing them with a new jargon. Such deep change increases the necessity for routinised practice, a thicker professional skin and a higher threshold of response. Such pressures marry-up with anxiety generated by the distressing nature of the primary work task itself, which, for social workers, is coping with the extremes of the human condition: disability, mental illness, deprivation, dishonesty, cruelty, pride, prejudice, ageing and death, all in the context of human dynamics of a powerful kind. It is hardly surprising that extraordinary need eventually becomes treated as mundane and achieves less significance in everyday practice. This process of 'banalisation' has been described graphically in relation to professionals who become capable of turning a blind eye to child abuse by Hadjiiski (1987; Hadjiiski *et al.* 1985; and below), but applies to other client groups as well, notably to people with disabilities, elders and people with mental health problems.

The Social Defences of the Bureauprofessional
THE HIERARCHICAL CRADLE

Menzies' (1959) classic paper on the social defences at work in the nursing hierarchy of a teaching hospital is highly relevant to the state of mind generated by the working context of the bureauprofessional and described above. Menzies describes how anxiety associated with intimate and, sometimes, traumatic nursing care and treatment is controlled by a rigid demarcation of roles and tasks, an over-concern with hierarchy and a diffusion of responsibility with endless checking and cross-checking. Thus anxiety is diverted from the primary task of care and treatment onto the guidelines and checking systems within the hierarchy. Menzies explains how individual thought and initiative are stifled in this situation and staff become over-dependent on rules and routine so that they are blind or ineffectual in situations to which, as individuals, they would respond more intelligently (Miller 1974).

Listening to social workers employed as care managers and senior care managers in relation to elders or adults with disabilities, or to those in the fields of child protection or mental health, Menzies' description speaks volumes. Even with their new masks and aliases affixed, social workers still recognise that guidelines, eligibility criteria and service contracts have often taken the place of the exercise of individual professional knowledge and skill. They also recognise that management through guidelines is no substitute for individual professional judgement and the kind of client-specific inter-agency collaboration that is required in each field of social work practice. As Sheldon (1997) said in a recent BASW London Branch meeting, 'you have to keep your social work knowledge and human skills secret, don't you?' His point was proven when a care team manager stated on a training day that needs assessment following the death of a spouse aged 83 and a marriage of over 60 years could not and must not include counselling which must 'if needed' be costed as part of the care package. The social work care manager in these terms must simply enter, assess and report, but must not 'become involved'.

THE ANTI-PROFESSIONAL TENDENCY

Yet it is not fair simply to hold the under-resourced, bureaucratic context of social services and other large organisational systems responsible for the constraints on quality practice. 'Social workers have at best been somewhat uneasy with what is perceived as the elitism of professional status and at worst, have attacked the idea of individual excellence with which it was felt to be linked' (Pietroni, M. 1995, p.34).

Collective and structural analyses of social deprivation and need were more fashionable in the 1970s and early 1980s. Skilled individual assessment and carefully tailored services were often seen as a soft option that ran the risk of enabling clients who were disadvantaged by an unjust system to adapt to it. Individual professionalism became an unfashionable idea and was considered 'élitist', probably the worst insult that social workers could at that time deliver against their own in order to ensure strong group norms of conformity and equality.

This 'anti-professional tendency' culminated in social work becoming the leading voice in the care sector on 'equal opps' as it became known. At best, this tendency undid the residues in social work of a nineteenth century form of social patronage 'from on high' and the more inappropriate excesses of professionalism, particularly that version of psychodynamic social work which drew too heavily on archaic forms of the Freudian 'blank screen' approach to individual sessions with clients. At worst, the anti-professional tendency produced a sheep-like culture of political correctness, as shallow in its conceptualisation as it was deeply embedded in its own prejudices.

At best or worst, the anti-professional and anti-individualist tendencies inhibited explorations of complex individual experience and perception which are at the heart of the project in observational study.

Complexity can be opened up in slow motion in an observation seminar. Each strand of what is experienced and subsequently felt or thought becomes available for reflection and discussion. A range of different views on the experience can be brought to bear and a variety of alternative interpretations can be considered. This depth of discussion also allows emotion and cognition to meet up. Students describe how increasing observational skill prevents any tendency toward simplistic or snap judgements from taking over and, because they observe the same individual or agency over time, they become aware of the complex interactions at work.

'THE CRADLE' OF GROUP MEMBERSHIP

As stated earlier, it has been suggested by Kristeva (1988) that the groups to which we belong (for example, our professional networks and the bureaucracies which employ us) are too often like a 'cradle' which lull us into a false state of child-like dependency and constrict our capacity for independent (and implicitly adult) thought and judgement. For this reason, she suggests, the identity conferred by any group is likely to be a crucial political and ethical issue (Oliver 1993). How can democratisation work and tolerance and understanding increase, she asks, unless we can draw on a range of identity-perspectives that use different language codes and are embedded in different cultures? Kristeva's position is radically opposed to the cruder forms of pressure toward group conformity which are a feature of any professional membership system, including social work.

Kristeva therefore suggests that it is important to draw one's identity from membership of several groups with contrasting beliefs and different languages. In this way, we can not only explore, we can even enjoy the otherwise confusing cross-currents using a wider range of language and interpretation than if we give our allegiance to one group only.

Observational study carried out in a multi-professional learning group can, therefore, in these terms, offer emancipation at many levels and has the potential to become a powerful learning event. Students relinquish the habitual blind spots established as a result of uni-professional basic training and, in part, as a result of the early socialisation processes of joining an organisation and establishing professional group membership (see Figure 5.7). At a recent research and evaluation day, students described their judgements becoming less routine whilst their capacity to hold in mind alternative and contradictory interpretations increased. If this re-learning experience takes place in a multiprofessional learning group, students hear the very different ways in which other members of the multiprofessional network interpret similar phenomena. Therefore, professional identity

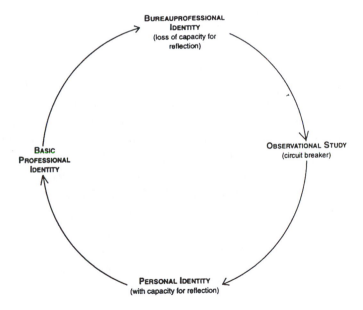

Figure 5.7: Breaking the bureauprofessional circuit

becomes more flexible, more mature, more continuously questioning and more deeply human.

BANALISATION

What effect does the 'cradling' of the professional group membership have in practice? Here Hadjiiski's (1987; Hadjiiski *et al.* 1985) concept of 'banalisation' is useful. Defined above as the mental numbness that the bureauprofessional is forced to develop as a result of the organisational context and human content of their work, this concept was described first in relation to abused and neglected children. Hadjiiski describes the process by which something horrific is treated as 'banal' (i.e. mundane) and something which is urgent attracts either no response or one which is limited, routine and often prescribed from above.

The pain generated by working as a professional with families involved in abusive relationships is so impossible to bear, Hadjiiski argues, that the professional concerned tends to turn away defensively rather than face that pain. In part, this may lead to a position where the neglect or abuse of the child goes unrecognised because of the emotional pain associated with it. Instead, the professional excuses the neglect, or rationalises it, and so the process of banalisation is complete. In this way, the child who is subject to neglect may also be ignored.

Bureaucratised care systems often remove the capacity to face pain and need in a critical and thoughtful way since the bureacracy is concerned with regulation and standardisation and is, by definition, antipathetic to critical thought. The professional's capacity for independent critical thought and emotional response is also numbed by repeated involvement with disturbing front-line situations. When both intellect and emotion are numbed, Hadjiiski argues, 'banalisation' is virtually inevitable. Then risk can go unnoticed and defensive professional habits and organisational routines prevail.

Observational study helps to undo this banalisation and increases the resilience of professionals in the face of interminable human pain and need. By helping to establish a disciplined inner space in each individual professional where experience is 'chewed over' and a range of other theoretical and professional viewpoints become part of the inner digestive process, reflective practice can be sustained.

Educational Issues

MAIN EDUCATIONAL AIM: PERSPECTIVE TRANSFORMATION

One of the benefits of direct observational study of an individual client, or an organisation at work, is that it requires the experienced bureauprofessional to explore and experiment with new perspectives by stepping outside of their usual role, organisational framework and state of mind. Since this exploration takes place without the everyday burdens of professional responsibility and accountability, a change of perspective can safely occur.

This kind of 'perspective transformation' is considered a necessary characteristic of advanced level education (Mezirow 1981). As a result, awareness of client need is increased and sensitivity to the unhelpful aspects of the system at work are enhanced. The observer usually finds a new perspective which is neither that of the 'bureau' nor that of their own profession but which is uniquely their own. That perspective seems to be more deeply rooted in their own personal identity and values, and whilst it is both critical and analytical, it feels to those that witness the change more deeply human. Students describe recovering their sense of human as opposed to professional priorities and a strengthened capacity for individual judgement and thought. Awareness of the emotional and ethical issues present in the situation seem to become available for consideration without the intrusion of habitual social defences which are part of any professional framework.

INTER-PROFESSIONAL UNDERSTANDING

The observer also becomes aware of the wider inter-professional and inter-agency environment which the constricting social defences of the bureauprofessional role had previously obscured. Repeated social services and Department of Health inquiry reports have called for improved inter-professional and inter-agency communication, but these are difficult to achieve in practice without a lively sense of how vital such collaboration is to the interests of the client. The cradling effect of 'membership' of a complex and, often, dehumanising bureauprofessional system tends to diffuse that vitality. Observation enhances it.

It has been demonstrated that the, often, negative perceptions held by different professionals of each other are developed early in training and go on to affect inter-professional relations and collaboration in practice (Pietroni, P.C.P. 1991). Yet in a system of health and social care which depends upon professionals working collaboratively within various forms of organisation, these identities are sometimes rigid and unhelpful. Ultimately then, as Kristeva (1988) concludes, innovation and creativity depend on freedom from belonging too strictly to any single group and sign system.

STAFF AND STUDENT DEVELOPMENT: RELINQUISHING THEORY AND FINDING A METHOD

Initially, all new academic staff teaching on other modules on the MA programme were asked to carry out at least one observation, either of an individual or of an organisation. These observations were carried out, broadly speaking, within a flexible form of the Tavistock psychodynamic model. Staff observed individuals and organisations at work and discussed their prior expectations and experience as they did so. Since that time, the observational staff team itself has continued to develop with the help of module leaders – Meira Likierman 1992–4 and Tony McCaffrey 1995–97, the latter using his triple background in anthropology, social work and psychotherapy to good effect.

It is difficult, however, to find staff with sufficient range of experience and theoretical knowledge in the field of observational study. A research training brings knowledge of observation, participant or non-participant, used as a research method and an anthropological perspective ensures that theoretical issues of meaning, both cultural and linguistic, can be addressed. A psychodynamic perspective brings a rigorous method of both observation and reflection. Few staff, however, have a grounding in all three perspectives.

The UW staff team have found that reviewing, with each other and with students, the texts and the actual process of writing up observations circumvents some of these theoretical and methodological problems. Their work with students (some of whom are used to writing minimalist impersonal notes) has been beneficial all round. The inter-professional aspects of recording can come to the fore and the GPs' inner pattern of 'six minutes for the patient' can stand in contrast to the practical 'no-nonsense' approach of the nurses and the 'long-windedness' of the social workers. Didacticism can be avoided, whilst each stage in the process of observation – emotional impact, reflection, interpretation and, most particularly, construction of meaning and choice of language – become available for consideration. Although the backdrop is a recognition of the complexity of observational method and theory, simplicity is sustained by working in ordinary language at reviewing the text and the writing process itself (Scott 1997).

It is, however, a considerable challenge to bring together different theoretical and methodological traditions and then to be able to think flexibly and yet rigorously across them. In this we have only just begun.

Summary and Implications

Observational learning can open up new layers of meaning in the basic professional identity of the individual health or social care practitioner. At the same time, a more critical perspective on the prevailing cultures and practices in large employing organisations is established. The observational learning experience also seems to enable course members to become emancipated from the role constrictions and peer group pressures that came with initial membership of their core professional group. Greater professional autonomy is achieved and the capacity for human creativity, so essential to reflective practice, recovers. Perhaps even more significant in these days of evidence-based practice, students report how observational study helps them to access a new form of evidence that can be used to inform assessments of risk and need, court reports, new training exercises or staff development. They feel more confident as a result.

In sum, observational study seems to provide a means of transcending individual professional identities established during basic training whilst generating a shared learning culture and a commitment to inter-professional understanding. The outcome seems to be a deeper understanding of complex advanced practice that is as human as it is rigorous.

References

Argyris, C. and Schön, D. (1974) *Theory in Practice: Increasing Professional Effectiveness.* San Francisco and London: Jossey Bass.

Balint, E. and Norrell, J. (1973) *Six Minutes for the Patient: Interventions in General Practice Consultation.* London: Tavistock Publications.

Bick, E. (1968) 'The experience of skin in early object relations.' *International Journal of Psychoanalysis 49,* 484–6.

Bion, W. (1961) *Experiences in Groups.* London: Tavistock Publications.

Bridge Consultancy (1997) *The Inquiry into the Circumstances of the Death of Ricky Neave.* Cambridge: Cambridge Social Services.

DoH (1983) *The Mental Health Act 1983.* London: HMSO.

DoH (1989) *The Children Act 1989.* London: HMSO.

DoH (1990) *The National Health Service and Community Care Act 1990.* London: HMSO.

DoH (1991) *The Patient's Charter*. London: HMSO.

Fermie, P. (1994) *Observational Study Paper: MA in Community and Primary Health Care*. London: University of Westminster.

Griffiths, Sir R. (1989) *Community Care: An Agenda for Action*. London: HMSO.

Hadjiiski, E. (1987) 'On first contact with child abuse and neglect.' *Journal of Social Work Practice 3*, 1, 31–37.

Hadjiiski, E., Agostini, D., Dardel, F. and Thouvenin, C. (1985) *Du Cri au Silence: Contribution à L' Étude des Attitudes des Intervenants Médico-Sociaux Face à L'Enfant Victime de Mauvais Traitements*. Vanves: Centre Technique National d'Études et de Recherches.

Kristeva, J. (1988) *Desire in Language: A Semiotic Approach to Literature and Art*. New York: Columbia University Press.

Leathard, A. (ed) (1995) *Going Interprofessional: Working Together for Health and Welfare*. London: Routledge.

MCT (Marylebone Centre Trust) (1991) *Working Principles of the Education and Training Unit*. London: MCT.

Menzies, I.E.P. (1959) *The Functioning of Social Systems as a Defence Against Anxiety: a Case Study of the Nursing Hierarchy in a Teaching Hospital*. London: Tavistock Pamphlet.

Mezirow, J. (1981) 'A critical theory of adult learning and education.' *Adult Education. Adult Education of the USA 32*, 1, 3–24.

Miller, M. (1974) 'Residential care: some thoughts and speculations on the literature.' *Social Work Today, 5*, 9, 259–265.

Oliver, K. (1993) *Reading Kristeva: Unravelling the Double-Bind*. Bloomington and Indianapolis: Indiana University Press.

Pietroni, M. (1992) *MA in Community and Primary Health Care: Towards Reflective Practice. Validation Document*. University of Westminster.

Pietroni, M. (1995) 'The nature and aims of professional education for social workers: a postmodern perspective.' In M. Yelloly and M. Henkel (eds) *Learning and Teaching in Social Work: Towards Reflective Practice*. London: Jessica Kingsley Publishers.

Pietroni, P.C.P. (1991) 'Stereotypes or archetypes? A study of perceptions amongst health-care students.' *Journal of Social Work Practice 5*, 1, 61–69.

Pietroni, P.C.P. (1996) *A Primary Care Led NHS: Trick or Treat? Inaugural Professorial Lecture*. Centre for Community Care and Primary Health, University of Westminster.

Schön, D. (1983) *The Reflective Practitioner: How Professionals Think in Action*. New York: Basic Books.

Schön, D. (1987) *Educating the Reflective Practitioner: Toward a New Design for Teaching and Learning in the Profession*. San Francisco: Jossey Bass.

Schön, D. (1992) 'The crisis of professional knowledge and the pursuit of an epistemology of practice.' *Journal of Interprofessional Care 6*, 1, 49–63.

Scott, A. (1997) Personal communication to the author.

Sheldon, B. (1997) *The Future of Social Work Education*. London: BASW Branch Meeting.

Spratley, J. and Pietroni, M. (1992) *Creative Collaboration: Interprofessional Learning Priorities in Primary Health and Community Care*. London: Marylebone Centre Trust/CCETSW.

Thomas, J. (1995) *Observational Study Paper: MA in Community and Primary Health Care: Towards Reflective Practice.* London: University of Westminster.

CHAPTER SIX

Holding a Mirror to the Institution
Observation and the Training of Approved Social Workers

Hazelanne Lewis

Approved Social Workers (ASWs) are required to exercise finely tuned judgements which have significant implications for clients. Frequently, ASWs are required to make measured decisions in circumstances which are fraught, complex and uncertain. The capacity to reflect critically upon one's practice in such circumstances and make connections with previous experience, knowledge and research is a desired attribute of the ASW. Observation, modelled on the ideas of the Tavistock Clinic, has been recognised as an important vehicle for facilitating reflective practice. This model has been incorporated into a specific approved social worker training programme and the focus switched from the observation of an individual to the observation of an acute psychiatric ward. This chapter explores the development and outcome of this initiative for the professional development of ASWs.

Mental Health: Changing Perspectives

Under the 1983 Mental Health Act (DoH 1983) doctors have a duty to examine the person and decide whether or not he or she is suffering from a mental disorder, within the meaning of the Act, of a nature or a degree which warrants detention in hospital. The ASW has the task of deciding whether, given the two medical recommendations, the person is suffering from a mental illness, and that there are no appropriate alternatives to hospital, an application should be made to detain the person in hospital (DoH and Welsh Office 1993). The different perspectives and responsibilities of ASWs and doctors are a potential source of conflict. The power of the ASW to refuse to apply for a person's admission was initially given to workers who had no formally assessed post-qualification training. Indeed, in the initial working years of the 1983 Mental Health Act many ASWs had only a few weeks' training. Even if doctors had not traditionally considered themselves to be in a position of specialist knowledge and power, it would have been difficult for them with six years' assessed post-graduate training and experience to accept having their judgement turned down by someone with a few weeks' post-qualification training and as little as two years' working experience (DoH 1983). CCETSW's development of the formal 60-day assessed ASW course can be seen as an attempt to improve the professional status of ASWs.

CCETSW has chosen to have the assessment carried out on the National Vocational Qualification (NVQ) competency model rather than the traditional examinations model. Trainees are required to submit a portfolio in which they have to evidence the 38 CCETSW designated competencies. If the portfolio meets the required standard, trainees are recommended to be warranted under the procedures of their employing authorities. In many ASW programmes trainees are expected to discuss the experience of assessment and admission to hospital with a user. In addition to this, the programme described in this chapter uses a model of observational placement similar to that of the Marylebone Institute at Westminster University, which I will discuss later in this chapter. Trainees are asked to observe an acute psychiatric ward.

Social workers are trained to take the social environment into account. They often see doctors as considering only the areas of biological aspects of malfunctioning in a person and labelling him or her as ill when social circumstances can produce a similar effect. Brown and Harris's (1978) study of socially deprived women in Southwark is a good illustration of this. Doctors see themselves as reaching their diagnosis through drawing on informed practice based on scientific evidence and taking the whole person into account (Tyrer and Steinberg 1994). In the 1960s the work of Szaz (1961), Goffman (1961) and Laing (1967) widened thinking about causes and climates leading to mental illness. Their views fitted in well with the prevalent thinking about social and power inequalities perpetuating oppression and were adopted by many social scientists (Busfield 1996). The Mental Health Act 1983 uses the words 'mental disorder' in its definition; doctors and the public refer to mental illness. The latter is a label which implies the need for treatment rather than the need to consider the wider social issues that might enable an easing of the disorder. The two different approaches led to challenges to doctors' power to diagnose and treat. The developing civil liberties movement encouraged users of the service to find ways to have their experiences of the mental health care system heard and understood. This widened the split. It should be noted that over the past decade the perception of ASWs to the implementation of the 1983 Mental Health Act (MHA) has shifted. In the early days, many ASW practitioners felt that the emphasis was on ensuring civil liberties. Now, many practitioners feel that emphasis has shifted to risk assessment and risk minimisation.

The twentieth century has seen a move away from the 'out of sight out of mind' Victorian asylums philosophy to caring for people in the community. The development of neuroleptic drugs from the middle of the century gave psychiatrists new ways of caring for mentally disordered people. The movement of patients out of the hospitals into, first, local psychiatric units and then the community has been gradual, with discussion focusing on philosophy of care and finance. The current emphasis on caring for people in the community and the growth of multi-disciplinary teams has enhanced the development of common skills and tasks among the care professionals as well as furthering the understanding of the different skills and tasks of professionals. Joint training on issues such as risk assessment and the Care Programme Approach (CPA) has furthered this understanding (DoH 1990b).

The Care Programme Approach was informed by the models of care management that began emerging in the United States from the mid-1970s onwards. These had developed in an attempt to provide a comprehensive service to people with severe mental health problems who were increasingly drifting into homelessness and prison, with hospital being seen as a better option. Services became more specialised but not more integrated. The 1972 Seebohm reorganisation of social services into teams of generic workers added to the perception of a lack of an integrated mental health service in the UK. The 'revolving door' phenomenon increased as some of the mentally disordered population appeared to find hospitalisation preferable to abandonment in the community.

By the beginning of the 1990s, many large psychiatric hospitals had either closed or had run down their patient numbers. Since the paper *Caring for People* (DoH/SSI 1990), the thrust of government policy has been increasingly away from hospitals. The National Health Service and Community Care Act 1990 (DoH 1990a) laid the ground rules for assessing and meeting needs in the community. Concurrent with the implementation of the National Health Service and Community Care Act 1990 came the move back to specialism in social work. Experience in the social services was that doctrinal pronouncements about care of people in the community were not matched by financial investment. Many multi-disciplinary teams were expected to support people in the community without the resources to offer this support. The shift away from local authority support to commissioning support from private and voluntary sectors at first met with resistance. Then financial pressure from government forced the shift. In some areas there has been innovative development of services, in others not. Social workers are seeing many of their traditional roles being taken over by community support workers, leaving them with the social policing and care management role. Psychiatrists, too, have seen their traditional power bases eroded as the capacity to purchase services has been given to General Practitioners. The latter are perceived as frequently preferring to purchase Community Psychiatric Nurses' (CPN) services for the worried well rather than for the seriously and enduringly mentally ill (Gournay and Brooking 1995).

This was the background to the different stances which ASWs and doctors frequently took when assessing someone thought to be suffering from a mental disorder. The initial interpretation of the Act was to promote civil liberty. The criteria for the admission sections of the Mental Health Act (2 and 3) ('of nature or degree which warrants detention in hospital...ought to be so detained in the interests of his health or safety or with a view to the protection of other persons') were interpreted as 'in the interests of his health and safety or with a view to the protection of other persons'. It was only when the Mental Health Act Commission's new Code of Practice came out in 1993, with the clear guidance on admission for the sake of a person's health, that practice started changing. It was soon after this that the emphasis in mental health care moved from civil liberties to risk containment, hastened by public outcry over Clunis and others (Ritchie, Dick and Lingham 1994). However, it might be fair to say that many social work practitioners feel that the move in practice is ahead of that of many DipSW courses where the emphasis is still on civil liberties (Lingham 1997). This can present practising social workers with dilemmas as they find the work expected from them at odds with their training and with the philosophy that made them enter social work. The development of user advocacy movements has created further dilemmas for social workers. In the case of ASWs, the power to deprive someone of their liberty based not on a trial but on two medical recommendations and the ASW's application can be experienced as further removing the social workers from the desire to work in a way that empowers clients.

Background to the Candidates

Social workers on the Hertfordshire/Barnet Approved Social Work Programme come from one county, one outer London borough and one inner London borough. The social workers accepted onto the approved social work course are two years' post-qualification and usually have heavy caseloads. All are expected to be working with mentally ill clients. Most work in mental health teams. The county has a large number of learning disabled clients and social workers from these multi-disciplinary teams are accepted onto the course. All three local authorities have specialist workers with the elderly mentally ill who are also accepted onto the course. Prior to coming onto the course, all social workers are asked to shadow two assessments for admission to hospital under the Mental Health Act. Those not working in a mental health team are asked to shadow three. The preparation for coming on the course caused problems for the trainees' managers, who were reluctant to lose working time from the trainees. Time off to meet the pre-course requirements is time off from a caseload that needs to be tidied up and run down prior to trainees leaving work for three months. In addition, trainees were expected to continue with normal duty work. Indeed, one trainee was given a new case in her last week at work before going on the course.

Parkinson and Thompson (forthcoming) consider whether ASWs are more likely to seek and secure space for reflecting on their practice if they are helped to develop their reflective ability during their ASW training. The CCETSW competencies emphasise the importance of being reflective when practising as an ASW. Schön (1987, 1993) writes of how the enabling of professionals to make decisions under conditions of uncertainty is necessary to shape professional identity – that sometimes the only possibility of describing knowledge is through observing and reflecting on actions. CCETSW looks at the need to evaluate one's own practice, knowledge and values with others; to review and appraise current research findings and to integrate well-tested outcomes into practice. It is through this process of evaluation, review and integration that a practitioner can move from being 'competent' to 'artistry'.

It was in an attempt to shift the social workers from being pressurised professionals to becoming reflective practitioners that trainees were asked to carry out observations in an acute psychiatric unit. The observations would also inform their practice as ASWs and give them greater understanding of the needs of ward staff as well as the likely care, treatment and experiences of patients on the ward. Social workers usually only have contact with a client when they have a task to perform. Observing clients in an in-patient setting without having a role enables candidates to have different experiences from those in their normal professional life. Just observing would, it was hoped, give an insight to the feelings clients might have about their care. The time set aside for writing up their observations, discussing them and later writing up their reflections on their observations would encourage their develop-ment as a reflective practitioner.

Initially, the observation model used was based on that developed in infant observation where a trainee observes the infant for one hour a week and writes up the observations, which are then presented to a seminar group, which helps with the process of reflecting on what has been observed (Hunt 1995; Trowell and Miles 1991). To this model the Marylebone Centre Trust at the University of Westminster added a sequence on observing institutions. On the course described here, trainees were asked to arrange to observe all aspects of life on an acute psychiatric ward for one hour a week for five weeks and to write up their observations after the hour had ended. This took place before the beginning of the course. Once the course had started, trainees were asked to present their observations in small groups for discussion and reflection upon the experience. They were advised to choose a ward on which they did not normally work.

Feedback from trainees established that by only observing once a week without the opportunity to present their observations for discussion between sessions, it was difficult to maintain the flow of concentration. Because of work commitments, some trainees had to observe everyday for a week and reported finding this much easier. The managers also appeared more sympathetic to the observations being organised in this way. As a result of this, the observation format was changed for the whole group. Now, trainees are asked to arrange to spend one hour a day, preferably the same hour, for five days observing an acute psychiatric ward. It would have been ideal for trainees to observe whilst on the course with concurrent seminars. Currently, time available precludes this possibility.

In keeping with the Tavistock model of observation, trainees are asked not to initiate conversation but are allowed to respond if approached. Trainees are not supposed to take notes while observing but are asked to write up what they observed after leaving the unit. After the course starts, the experience of being an observer is discussed and candidates are asked to reflect on their observations. The suggested areas they are asked to consider are:

- ambience
- communication – between staff and staff, staff and patients, patients and patients
- the feelings the observer has of patients' understanding of people's roles
- stress – on staff, on patients, on visitors
- power and oppression
- how they felt as observers
- anything else they feel relevant
- how they will apply what they have learnt.

On the first occasion trainees on the course were asked to do this, most of the acute psychiatric units queried the propriety of the request and asked for further explanations. Candidates were furnished with a letter explaining that they were there to learn about the stress on staff working in the unit. Subsequently, most of the units appeared to accept the requests without anxiety. However, one trainee had to try three different units before she was allowed to observe. In all, 15 different units have been observed. It was arranged that trainees would be introduced to staff and patients at the first session. In some cases this did happen, with trainees being introduced at the ward community meeting and a discussion of their role ensuing. In other cases, the manager who agreed to the observations was away and did not appear to have informed anyone else. This left trainees having to justify their presence to duty staff and explain why they were there and what they wanted to learn from patients.

Insights from Observation

The Role of the Observer

All trainees found taking up the role of an observer difficult. It seemed that their identity was lost when they had no focus of being in a 'work' role. Social workers are used to seeing clients for focused work; without a focus, the trainees complained of feeling 'bored', 'uneasy', 'that they were regarded with suspiciousness [sic] by patients'. Some were afraid of the potential violence of the patients. The enforced inactivity was found to be very difficult. Chiesa (1993) has written of how difficult it is to be an observer in this situation. He wonders whether the enforced inactivity and apparent boredom might hold fears of the observer's own madness for them. Some trainees were able to reflect on why they felt so uneasy, others not. From the reports, it seemed that the trainees went in looking for oppressive practice – which most found easily. Some appeared to identify with the patients but most found themselves divided between awareness of the difficulty of being a staff member working on the ward and acknowledging this difficulty. Trainees had difficulty acknowledging how their practice might be affected if they too had an eight-hour shift on the ward.

Ambience

All trainees commented on the ward environment. Some were favourably impressed by the physical environment but others felt that the poor state reflected the feelings of staff and patients on the ward. There appeared to be little attempt to separate out the feelings of trainees from their observations:

> The ceiling was low which I felt was a bit oppressive. There were several drawings and paintings done by patients stuck on walls, also, some poems and other 'words of wisdom' which meant something special to someone, I assumed.
>
> The ward was a very gloomy place, the day room was grubby and used as a walk through corridor by staff and patients... When there was hardly anyone in the room it felt tense and uneasy. The stuffiness seemed overpowering at times.
>
> I realised how bleak and inhospitable a place it was in appearance. I found it under resourced both in terms of staff and equipment and this in itself caused difficulties and stress.

Some commented on the contrast between the new building in which they were observing and the oppressive atmosphere on the ward, others that the grubby old building increased the sense of oppression. For many, the realisation of how oppressive the atmosphere felt only came when they left the building at the end of their first observation: 'My own mood lifted as I left the ward'. Only four trainees felt that the ward they observed had a positive, friendly ambience.

Staff-To-Staff Communication

Communication was seen as the central area of care on the ward. Communication varied enormously within the wide range of units being observed. Greater differences were observed between staff-to-staff communication across the board than between staff-to-patient communication. In good units, where staff knew each other well, 'non-verbal communication was frequently employed to cue-in a colleague to the nuances of an unfolding situation'; 'I felt that the team was a very supportive and trusting team'.

These comments contrasted markedly with: 'Communication between staff in patient areas was sometimes loud and inappropriate'; '...staff seemed largely disengaged particularly in their attitude towards patients'; 'I was surprised at how little staff did communicate with each other and when they did in the office it seemed as though they were shouting not talking to each other'; 'four nurses sat outside the office, with clipboards, not communicating to each other or the patients'. This last observation was on a ward where all but one member of staff were new or agency or bank staff – one working on a psychiatric unit for the first time. On these wards a correspondingly low state of morale was noticed. Donati (1989) also writes of this low morale on under-resourced wards.

Some trainees were able to reflect on the pressures on staff in a short-staffed unit with a high number of disturbed patients when a new patient was admitted by an ASW. They were able to transfer their reflections to their practice when it came to thinking about what staff would need from an admitting ASW in terms of information when writing their portfolios.

Many of the trainees commented on the hierarchy of staff coming to the ward. It was noticed that all staff who came to the ward expected nurses to give them immediate attention. Trainees felt that doctors, in particular consultants, were given the most immediate attention. Some resented this, others acknowledged that it was the Responsible Medical Officer (RMO) who had the power to discharge patients from the ward. All noticed the powerlessness of patients.

Staff–Patient Communication

On the whole, trainees observed that most staff–patient communication was initiated by patients. There was a link between the poor communication between staff and staff and that between staff and patients. On some wards, particularly those with a high number of agency staff, staff seemed to cling to their tasks rather than be open to engage in conversations with patients. This could be seen as a defence against their anxiety at working in a strange situation and with unpredictable, severely mentally ill patients (Donati 1989; Menzies 1959): 'Patients mostly initiated communication with staff, either verbally or by acting out'; 'Communication between staff and patients appeared only to take place when it was essential'; 'One of the patients commented to me that "nothing goes on around here except meals, medication and occupational therapy"'; 'There seemed to be no equitable nursing time for patients. Patients who "acted up" got more attention from nursing staff'.

Communication was seen to be best at medication rounds, when, on the wards where there was good communication, nurses seized the opportunity to have informal conversations. It was also observed that on most wards, patients' affairs would be discussed with them in front of other patients, thus ignoring the need for confidentiality. However, on four wards the trainees were impressed that the care staff took to treat patients with dignity and respect their confidentiality. On some wards a regular nurse coming on duty would go round greeting everyone and asking how they were.

What was highlighted was the number of units with agency staff who were new to the ward as well as to the patients. As already mentioned, it was on these wards that staff–patient communication was seen to be particularly poor. One trainee first observed on a ward which did not operate a nurse key-worker system for its patients and then worked on one that did during his placement. Nursing staff felt that the key-worker system enabled them to give more individual time to patients and provided an easier structure for patients to cope with. The trainee found that, even with a key-worker, patients felt that they did not receive 'talking time' from the nurses. 'Talking time' was seen as the most important area of care wanted by the users who came in as trainers on the course.

On several wards the domestic was seen as the one who communicated in the most relaxed manner with patients. Nursing assistants were not seen in as favourable a light. This may be because in wards with a mixed acute and elderly mentally ill population they were given the task of caring for and cleaning up incontinent, older people. This was not seen as a desirable job. 'The older patients were treated as deaf, blind and stupid by these staff'.

Trainees observed that it was the lower status nurses who usually spent most time with patients. Some built up a status picture of the regular inhabitants on the ward, with older patients at the bottom of the hierarchy and the charge nurse at the top. 'Communication between patients was also governed by hierarchy'.

Trainees who showed good reflective ability throughout their portfolios were the ones who showed an awareness of how the stress on the nurses led to behaviour which required a denial of nurses' feelings of distress: 'I became aware of the impact of constant daily contact with this mental pain on nursing staff'.

Communication Between Patients and Patients

As with the communication between staff and staff and staff and patients, so trainees observed that it was on those wards where there was good staff-to-staff communication that there was also good patient-to-patient communication: 'Much patient to patient re-assurance and emotional support was to be observed'. The same trainee had also observed: 'Staff were also specially sensitive about dealing with individual problems outside the day room on a 1:1 basis because of issues of dignity'. This contrasts strongly with: 'I saw little communication between staff and patients except in a practical sense' and 'Communication between patients was very limited'.

Trainees observed different levels of communication between patients. Those who were confined to the ward and were dependent on others buying things, usually cigarettes, for them had to find ways of communicating with fellow patients that would result in someone going to the shops on their behalf. 'The exchanges that I observed were quite fraught with anger and frustration particularly with those confined to the ward'.

There was little linking of the behaviour of the powerless, confined patient dependent on nicotine with the threats of violence and the power hierarchy within the ward. The hierarchy already commented upon was noticed but not always analysed by trainees. They were aware that the fitter, frequently younger, male patients tended to be more powerful on the ward. Powerful females could also be near the top of the hierarchy.

It was noticeable that patients would sit in the room with the TV and passively watch television. Many observed that the TV formed a backdrop to the events on the ward.

The institutionalisation of the patients and how this affected communication was commented upon by some trainees: 'Certain positions were more prized than others. Some of the more assertive seemed to claim these as their own. One woman in particular moved another patient from "her seat" glowering in the other person's direction until she moved'. One found that he too had become institutionalised by his fourth observation: 'I wondered if he bothered me because...his presence was upsetting my sense of the familiar'. He was able to use this to reflect on how in-patients would feel about the shifting familiarity: 'never being able to become comfortable with the people they shared their lives with, due to the high turn over of their hospitalised peers'.

Stress

The comments from trainees reflect the wide variation of stress level experienced by staff and patients: 'In my view the staff appeared to be competent, caring and at ease with the patients. This may have been a contributory factor to the relaxed environment'.

Not surprisingly, trainees found that those wards where there was a high level of agency staff appeared to be the wards where there was a high level of staff stress and, similarly, high stress on patients.

STRESS ON STAFF

'Having reflected back with some staff members of the team, it would seem that the time of day, numbers of staff on duty, numbers of new staff on any given shift, the numbers of new admissions and how settled patients are on the ward, all have an impact on stress levels on staff'.

Nurses are expected to carry out many different tasks during a shift, particularly on one when there is a ward round. They are frequently interrupted by visitors – either patients, other professionals or family and friends of patients. They care for people with different levels of mental illness and in varying levels of distress. The way they carry out their task is scrutinised by the Mental Health Act Commission. (Two of the wards being observed were visited by the Commission during an observation period.) This on its own is a daunting task. To add to the stress, most of the wards being observed had at least one agency staff and some had all agency nurses with the exception of the charge nurse. This means that staff who do not know each other or the patients and who may not have had up-to-date training in control and restraint techniques are expected to work in what can feel like a dangerous environment. This threat to safety was picked up by three of the trainees: 'I felt very threatened by the more acutely ill patients who would regularly invade my space and demand cigarettes from me'; 'At no time did I feel safe in my environment'.

No trainee mentioned the concept of the wards offering asylum. Relatively few were able to think about why staff sought safety in speaking to one another and sticking to the more concrete tasks. Few were able to think about how their own professional contact with clients was always task-focused and how they would feel if they had to draw on their own resources to be with patients for eight hours at a time. All acknowledged stress on staff but seemed to find it easier to focus on the stress on patients.

STRESS ON PATIENTS

Stress on patients was noted and considered by all trainees. Their main areas of focus were deprivation of liberty, the process of becoming a patient and loss of identity, the threat/tension on the ward, the increased tension/ excitement on ward round days, the lack of privacy, the powerlessness, the effect of heavy medication and the inadequacy of care offered to patients. Some were able to reflect on the effect of their observations on patients: 'Somehow I think that most people were genuinely uninterested or resented my being there'.

One considered the effect on an art therapy group of a nurse carrying out close observations: 'Everyone became twitchy as they all felt they were observed by the large woman at the door'.

Another area of stress for patients was the presence of visitors. There was little privacy for conversations. Those confined to the ward and sharing a dormitory had to deal with family stress in public. Little support was seen to be offered to distressed relatives.

As in all previous areas already discussed, where there were permanent staff who communicated well together, there appeared to be less stress on patients. It was on these wards that the fellowship between patients was observed to be strong: 'I was struck with the observation, that among all the trauma, the boredom, the tension and the unhappiness shared between patients, people were still able to establish friendships, show acts of kindness, and support each other in any number of ways'; 'These human contacts between patients gave me a sense of optimism about some of the therapeutic possibilities of hospitalisation'.

This was not the situation on many of the wards: 'The gloomy surroundings were stressful on their own, so was the lack of privacy, the knowledge that one was observed wherever one went and that conversations were aimed at one disclosing information about oneself with little in return'.

Stress on and oppression of patients were the commonest themes.

Issues of Power and Oppression

In their reports and reflections, oppression and powerlessness featured prominently. This is possibly because of the trainees' awareness that they would be the ones who would help deprive people of their liberty and bring them into what may be experienced as oppressive ward regimes.

Trainees' awareness of the oppression of patients was wide-ranging. Oppression was examined in three main areas: deprivation of liberty and lack of choice; power issues between staff and staff, between staff and patients and between patients and patients; and discrimination. In many ways it felt as though trainees found it easier to focus on anti-oppressive and anti-discriminatory issues for patients because these are in the normal practice of social work training and hence the trainees were on familiar ground. For some, these were the major areas of focus, with only lip service being paid to issues that affected staff: '...nurses still had to manage situations like this irrespective of their culture, gender, experience, training, familiarity with that ward and those colleagues, and the stress on them from their working conditions'.

This was tacked on at the end of reflections on observations in which no previous reference had been made to demands or stress on staff. It may be that it is easier to focus on patients for whom many trainees saw themselves as advocates rather than on 'oppressive' staff with whom patients may identify social workers. It is nursing staff who are responsible for detaining patients in such oppressive conditions but, ironically, it is ASWs who bring the patients into hospital. Some trainees who had not previously been aware of the oppressive implications of 'close observations' were shocked when they realised that 'the patient is closely observed at all times even when they go to the lavatory'.

A few trainees raised the issue of the ward being locked, even though not all patients were detained under the Mental Health Act: 'On several occasions I witnessed informal patients being told that they could not leave the ward.'

The difficulties staff had in preventing detained patients leaving the ward when they were so short-staffed was acknowledged by some. The belittling of patients, for example, as adults, being told when to get up, when to eat and go to bed and obtaining permission to go off the ward was noted by all.

Older patients were seen to be treated oppressively with little acknowledgement of their right to dignity. Interestingly, none of the trainees queried the suitability of treating the elderly mentally ill on the same ward as the 16- to 65-year-olds. Trainees showed more awareness of the need for women to have the opportunity for a separate ward or, at the least, for separated sleeping and toilet facilities which were not accessible to male patients. They were also aware of how the younger women in particular felt intimidated by the violent men.

Two trainees looked at carers and how their need for information and reassurance were not met on the ward. This was linked to the high number of agency staff.

Two trainees saw medication as linked to oppression. Both these trainees were the ones who felt most threatened while carrying out their observations. Only one was able to reflect on how nurses too might feel threatened while working on the ward. Other trainees commented more on the effect of medication on patients.

Issues of language, race and ethnicity were an important focus. To social workers used to working with interpreters it was difficult to see someone who did not appear to speak English being nursed without an interpreter being called in: 'Communication was primarily by gestures'.

Racist remarks by mentally ill patients posed dilemmas for trainees. One commented, after witnessing a hostile patient making racist comments to a doctor:

> I wondered what my reaction would be should I be confronted on a mental health assessment with that degree of hostility both as an ASW and with reference to my colour.

Discussion

The main advantage of observing an acute psychiatric unit over observing an individual is the breadth of learning that is available to the trainees. Trainees who had carried out observations had a greater awareness of the effects of admission on users, of the difficulties facing staff on the ward, of the importance of good communication and of oppression on the ward. As a result, some trainees had difficulty accepting the role of the ASW.

Initial Effects of Observations on Trainees

Social work training emphasises choice for people. ASW training is geared to helping social workers try to provide choices while assessing the risk to or by the client. The witnessing of the effects of depriving clients of their liberty was something that the trainees, as a group, found disturbing. The course emphasises a systematic approach to risk assessment, which is taught early in the course. Trainees are expected to assess risk using identified risk indicators, developed from research, to help them in reaching a decision. At the time, the tutor noticed a resistance to adopting a systematic approach which also examined risk in the past. It felt as though trainees were afraid of the consequences that seeing someone to be at risk would have for the client. Trainees appeared to have been perturbed by observing the powerlessness of clients in acute psychiatric wards. They showed difficulty in acknowledging the discrepancy between their choice to come on the course and their disquiet about their future use of the power of ASWs. If a group of ASW course co-ordinators meet, it is common to hear them complaining about how their trainees' behaviour appears to have regressed. This behaviour is frequently linked to trainees' anxiety about the power of the ASW. After about a month the anxiety usually abates as the trainees start to practice and gain confidence in their skills and judgement. Observation appeared to enable trainees to reflect in depth on their feelings. For some trainees, this appeared to mean that the period of regression continued longer. Trainees openly voiced their anxiety about the power of the ASW and their anxiety in using this power.

The Importance of Good Communication

Greater awareness of the need for gathering information and interviewing in an appropriate manner was noted. Some trainees appeared to feel obliged to ensure that all members of the assessing team interviewed the client at length to ensure that all factors were considered before admitting a client on a compulsory order. They were able to modify their practice after reflecting on how patients they observed on a ward spoke of feeling oppressed when having to undergo lengthy interviews. It was difficult for them to accept that they might be seen as oppressive.

There was bitter debate about the importance of providing the accepting nurse on the acute psychiatric unit with a written report. In their observations the trainees had recognised that for a stressed nurse to write down information obtained from an ASW would increase stress and might adversely affect patient care. The writing of a report could have been linked to power. If the ASW hands over the information, are they giving power over the patient to nurses? This links to the lack of comment in the observations of how it might feel to be a nurse working on an acute psychiatric ward and how relatively low in-patient nurses were perceived to be in the mental health professional hierarchy. Trainees were able to examine these issues and reflect on how their behaviour might be interpreted as defensive. Once the importance of leaving reports behind had been acknowledged, the reports written appeared more focused than those of previous years' trainees.

Oppression on the Ward

Trainees, having learnt about the experience patients have of care on wards, appeared to take a longer time to accept their role in taking people to hospital against their will. This may also link to the changing role of social workers in mental health teams mentioned earlier where the 'nice, supportive' part of social work has been hived off to the support workers, leaving the social workers as gatekeepers to resources and potential deprivers of liberty. It may also be that by observing, trainees got in touch with their own 'madness' and feared possible consequences for themselves. Certainly, the effect of the power of the ASW was a constant theme in the support groups' discussions.

Pierson (1997) urges 'a deliberative debate, a language that is capable of dialogue, a vocabulary that tolerates plural solutions and views about attaining the good society'. The experience of observation seemed particularly pertinent to facilitating reflection on the implications of admission or leaving someone in the community without adequate support. There was also less assumption of other professionals automatically following a 'medical model'. After initial anxiety, they appeared to be open to 'plural solutions'. Some trainees had difficulty matching their prospective new role with their desire to be trained as ASWs.

Trainees who had Difficulty Accepting the Role of the ASW

Carrying out the observations highlighted trainees who would continue to have problems exercising the power of the ASW. Busfield (1996) has noted how concepts of mental illness change over time. Certainly, some of the trainees needed to see mental illness resulting only from social pressures and their views were reinforced by their observations on the ward. Others who accepted wider models when considering causes of mental illness used their observations to inform their practice. They felt that they were able to use the knowledge gained to prepare clients more effectively for admission. In the future, observations could be used as a filter point indicating areas where those who are ambivalent about becoming an ASW might need extra support.

Conclusion

The format of observational placements in the training of approved social workers is still being developed. On the course discussed here the model of infant observation has been modified and applied to observation of adults in an institutional setting. The model has also proved to be a relevant tool for learning in post-qualifying education and training. Here it has made a specific contribution to the trainees' understanding of the complexity of the ASW's role. These contributions include a deeper understanding of mental illness, the life of institutions and professional processes in mental health. The trainees' comments demonstrate a heightened awareness of the significant part power relations play in carrying out their role and function. The opportunity to reflect in depth on these issues as part of a professional training programme hopefully enables the trainees to transfer ideas about competent and reflective practice into their working environment.

References

Brown, G.W. and Harris, T. (1978) *Social Origins of Depression: A Study of Psychiatric Disorder in Women.* London: Tavistock.

Busfield, J. (1996) *Men Women and Madness.* London: Macmillan Press.

CCETSW (1989, 1991, 1995) *Rules and Requirements for the Diploma in Social Work.* London: CCETSW.

Chiesa, M. (1993) 'At the border between institutionalization and community psychiatry: psychodynamic observations of a hospital admission ward.' *Free association 4*, 2, 241–263.

DoH (1983) *Mental Health Act 1983.* London: HMSO.

DoH (1990a) *The National Health Service and Community Care Act 1990.* London: HMSO.

DoH (1990b) *The Care Programme Approach for People with a Mental Illness Referred to the Specialist Psychiatric Services. (HC(90)23).* London: HMSO.

DoH/SSI (1990) *Caring for People: Community Care in the Next Decade and Beyond, Policy Guidance.* London: HMSO.

DoH and Welsh Office (1993) *Code of Practice. Mental Health Act 1983.* London: HMSO.

Donati, F. (1989) 'A psychodynamic observer in a chronic psychiatric ward.' *British Journal of Psychotherapy 5*, 3, 317–328.

Goffman, E. (1961) *Asylums.* Harmondsworth: Penguin.

Gournay, K. and Brooking, J. (1995) 'The community psychiatric nurse in primary care: an economic analysis.' *Journal of Advanced Nursing 22*, 4, 769–778.

Hunt, J. (1995) 'On the relevance of the observation of infants and young children to psychotherapeutic work with adults.' *Psychodynamic Counselling 1*, 4, 525–541.

Laing, R.D. (1967) *The Politics of Experience and the Bird of Paradise.* Harmondsworth: Penguin.

Lingham, R. (1997) Paper given at Launch Conference of Manchester University Introduction to Mental Health and Risk Assessment, London.

Menzies, I.E.P. (1959) *The Functioning of Social Systems as a Defence Against Anxiety: A Case Study of the Nursing Hierarchy in a Teaching Hospital.* London: Tavistock pamphlet.

Parkinson, C. and Thompson, P. (forthcoming) 'Uncertainty, mystery and doubts and approved social work training.' *Journal of Social Work Practice.*

Pierson, J. (1997) 'Form of words.' *Community Care,* 20–26 March, 28–29.

Ritchie, J., Dick, D. and Lingham, R. (1994) *The Report of the Inquiry into the Care and Treatment of Christopher Clunis.* London: HMSO.

Schön, D. (1987) *Educating the Reflective Practitioner: Towards a New Design for Teaching and Learning.* London: Jossey.

Schön, D. (1993) Reflective inquiry in social work practice. Unpublished paper, Centre for the study of Social Work Practice.

Szaz, T.S. (1961) *The Myth of Mental Illness.* New York: Hoeber-Harper.

Trowell, J. and Miles, G. (1991) 'The contribution of observation training to professional development in social work.' *Journal of Social Work Practice 5,* 1, 51–60.

Tyrer, P. and Steinberg, D. (1994) *Models for Mental Disorder.* Chichester: J.Wiley and Sons.

CHAPTER SEVEN

Observing Management

The Contribution of Observation to Management in the Personal Social Services

Patricia Kearney

> Light from the window behind Rivers's desk fell directly on to Sassoon's face... No twitches, jerks, blinks, no repeated ducking to avoid a long-exploded shell. His hands, doing complicated things with cup, saucer, plate, sandwiches, cake, sugar tongs and spoon, were perfectly steady. Rivers raised his own cup to his lips and smiled. One of the nice things about serving afternoon tea to newly arrived patients was that it made so many neurological tests redundant. (Barker 1992, p.10)

How do you feel reading this? Would you feel comfortable about looking at your clients like this? Would this sort of scrutiny be acceptable behaviour in a social work manager? The thought of observing clients or colleagues can make social workers feel uncomfortable. We are uneasy about the nature of our policing role and rightly consider a disease model of practice as an insufficient basis for professional practice. In this chapter I want to consider how the ideas around observation might contribute in particular to management within the personal social services. I suggest that they offer some ways out of the impasse we are in regarding the relationship between management and practice and some clarification of the kind of management models we want to use. I shall illustrate this thinking with some pictures of management practice from my work in the Development Unit at the National Institute for Social Work.

Observation and Social Work Practice

Within social work, the skills of observation are recognised as valuable although their application is often confined to work with families, particularly in the field of child protection. This is partly because observation skills are still largely characterised by their origins in the techniques of infant observation. That is, a development from within psychoanalytic discourse as a way of understanding developing interactions between the newborn and the parent (Miller *et al.* 1989).

In practice, observation skills have an undoubted value as part of social workers' assessments. An understanding of normal child development, its variations and its exceptions is vital to a social worker's assessment of a child's well-being, of his or her care needs and, subsequently, of the appropriateness of a child's parenting or other care. Observation skills are clearly especially helpful when assessing pre-verbal children.

Over time, that is by seeing a lot of children, a social worker will develop the skill to make such observations and know what conclusions to draw – is a child reaching the milestones appropriate for its age; what differences should you expect to see in children with learning difficulties or physical disabilities; does what you see concern you to look further? The seminal handbook *Protecting Children* (DoH 1988) is predicated on the application of observation skills; the Sheridan charts included in the book are a guide to precisely this establishing of normal child development.

It is striking, even in this seemingly unequivocal use of observation skills, that they are rarely a part of a social worker's basic training, in contrast with that of other professions where, for example, teachers and occupational therapists are trained to look at the behaviour of their subjects and to analyse it in the context of normal development and functioning. The importance of noting and understanding the range of 'ordinary' and particular behaviour is accepted as fundamental knowledge in a wide range of professions. Within the human sciences, anthropologists, doctors, nurses and teachers expect that if they look, they will learn: what they see informs them about what to do. In contrast, the reluctance to acknowledge observation expertise as part of the basic repertoire echoes throughout social work and, I would argue, has made it difficult for the skills and concepts of observation to be more widely applied. It reflects the tendency of workers, their agencies and the law to default towards an investigative and forensic mode.

The Department of Health's overview report, *Messages from Research* (HMSO 1995) has focused this debate within work with children and their families. It has recommended a greater emphasis on family support away from a narrowly defined investigative approach to child protection. The report references Parton's (1985) observation that 'Child maltreatment is not the same sort of phenomenon as whooping cough: it cannot be diagnosed with scientific measuring instruments. It is more like pornography, a socially constructed phenomenon which reflects values and opinions of particular times' (HMSO 1995, p.15).

Child protection work is only the most obvious demonstration of what social work is about – all of our professional concerns might be defined as social constructs and one of our major tasks is in operating within society's changing and contentious representations of these notions. Commenting on what we see becomes as difficult as it is unavoidable. How do we make sense of what we see when we are looking at social relationships and interactive behaviour and not at absolute conditions? For example, a broken hip is an unequivocal condition, but whether an elderly man in this condition needs the help of social services is probably entirely due to the state of his own social network and surroundings.

In these operating conditions we are wary of observation. Is it purely a forensic device? What authority do we have for determining the truth of what we see and acting upon it?

It is tempting, given these difficulties, to see things out of context, and it is right that social work is wary of doing this. However, this guardedness has 'pathologised' observation, strengthening the sense that it is somehow 'unfair', an unpermitted and devious look at how people 'give themselves away'. It seems antithetical to the profession's avowed emphasis on equality and supportive practice.

I suggest that this reluctance, in part, reveals our 'us and them' attitude to our clients – what may be allowable behaviour with them becomes unacceptable when it is applied to ourselves or our colleagues. We are hindered in applying observational skills outside certain specific areas of direct practice – it may just be permissible to look at failing parents but not at all permissible to look at our own practice and our management of practice. As Parton (1996) comments in his critique of *Messages from Research*: 'Remarkably, social work is virtually missing from the research... Social work is rarely studied in its own right. Yet social work and social services departments...virtually embody what it is to do child protection work and the tensions and contradictions involved' (p.8).

Observation and Family Therapy

It is helpful to look at the major evolution of observation that has been made in family therapy practice. This has met and addressed some of the same concerns raised within social work about the efficacy and ethics of observation. Family therapy has applied observation skills to an understanding of established interactions within family groups. Whilst medical practitioners within family therapy have brought a familiarity with diagnostic observation to this new practice, as Winnicott did to child psychotherapy, it has moved beyond a disease and diagnosis construct. Family therapy's use of observation has contributed to the understanding of family dynamics through a range of techniques, including non-participant observers, video and tape recording, that have heightened ways of seeing. The aim is to demonstrate to an outsider, the observer, and consequently show to the family themselves, the unique behaviour they had taken for granted. This new information about themselves aids the family in making positive changes to solve the problems they had previously found unsolvable.

Central to this major modification of observation have been the concepts of neutrality and feedback, both of which are informed by systems thinking. These are both rich concepts deserving discussion beyond the scope of this chapter, but I mention them here because I will return to them later as helpful notions in the management of social work.

'Neutrality' demands consideration of the observer's role. The neutrality of the family therapist is a reminder that she cannot know what only the family knows and is, consequently, required to be ignorant and, therefore, unavoidably curious. In turn, this allows the observer 'to develop the ability to suspend, at least temporarily, their agency task/function and to think outside their usual work... With this different perspective they can then step back inside their usual boundaries and translate this perspective into an action that is appropriate for their agency position' (Burnham and Harris 1988, p.69).

'Feedback' develops the systems theory notion of incorporating information into the system – it considers the system to include both the observer and those observed, with action creating re-action. That is, comment on and response to the observed behaviour, usually at the time of observation, so as to modify future behaviour. This is already very different from 'the observing gaze (that) refrains from intervening' described by Foucault (1973, p.107). This development opens up a rich field of speculation: can there be observation without immediate feedback? What is the position of the observer in order to give feedback? Issues of responsibility, moral stance and power are unavoidable aspects of such work.

Recent Developments in Social Work

Family therapy thinking shows that observation skills are not confined to a forensic or even mechanistic and pathologising practice. This has freed-up thinking about the uses of observation within social work, as shown by a number of recent developments. The first has been to take child and family observation seriously. That is, that the skills of observation require training and consultation over time if they are to be useful, fair and 'true'.

Trowell and Miles (1991) describe the observation training they set up as a response to the Cleveland inquiry. Their context is that of child protection but their analysis of the reluctance to use observation skills has useful wider applications in the field of social work and its management. They note:

- the stress involved in setting up a contract within which observation is allowable, 'fair' and equitable
- the anxiety felt by the worker because they are unclear about their observer role
- what they 'really see' can be distressing.

They emphasise the importance of ongoing consultation which 'provides a setting where anxiety and distress can be safely discussed, thus enabling learning to take root at a deeper level' (p.53).

A second area of development has been the growing emphasis on evidenced outcomes in social care training through the competency frameworks of National Vocational Qualifications and Management Charter Initiative standards. A similar emphasis in social worker training, particularly for practice teachers, has seen the growth of observation of both student and teacher as a normal part of their training.

Tanner and Le Riche (1995) have brought together both these strands, applying observation skills to a range of social work settings. Through their experience as social work teachers, they have developed a model that takes note of the 'hierarchy of power' manifested in the observation of practice teachers. They consider the negotiations necessary to ensure an 'equality' model of observation in such circumstances.

The potential applications of observation skills and thinking clearly have a wide application within social work practice and teaching. They provide a repertoire of assessment and action and, importantly, a conceptual framework that satisfies the profession's requirements for equity, probity and partnership. However, what has this to do with management?

Management and Practice in the Social Services

In the past decade the increasing and changing demands on statutory social care provision have had as great an impact on management as they have had on practice and on the training and professional development of social workers. There are major debates about the nature of management in such a time. General management principles have been applied throughout the public sector – education, health and policing as well as social care have been influenced (for a consideration of these developments see Pollit 1993).

Within social work the advent of community care legislation and changing financial structures, including devolved budgets and local government compulsory competitive tendering, have had their impact. Much has been written about the changes, welcomed and feared, to professional social work. Managers have faced similar challenges with the difference that these are against a background of neglected management training and development needs. What are the tasks of a modern manager and what are the skills they need to do their job?

The relationship between management and practice in social care has always been an ill-defined one. In a changing world, the nature of this relationship becomes even more acute. Social work and social care have always operated within complex bureaucracies. The tension between organisational management and professional activity is not a new one, as Parsloe (1996) notes: 'The danger...is that hierarchical structures invade professional areas and when this happens professional standards are likely to fall and, in addition, management will lose credibility even in those areas which can and should be managed' (pp.112–13).

These complexities are increasing as the mixed economy of care and the combined concerns of health and social care issues increase inter-agency working at all levels in social care agencies. Managers need technical and financial skills as never before. Can these be integrated with professional activity or will they exacerbate the division between the practice and management of social work even further?

Observation in Management

I suggest that the conceptual frameworks and particular skills of observation are one potential strand in closing the gap. They provide the chance to recognise the skills managers bring with them from practice. Moreover, they make explicit the fact that managers do influence practice quite directly by their own behaviour. This phenomenon is usually referred to as the culture of an organisation, and I shall come back to this notion later.

First, I want to look briefly at three areas: the refining of general management notions in the business world; organisational behaviour studies; and recent debate on supervision in the social services. These can all contribute to the application of observation skills in management.

The World of Business and Commerce

Riley (1997) comments on the irony that

> public sector managers are constantly being exhorted to look to the private sector for models of management expertise and professionalism. Social service managers daily manage much larger budgets, more complex operations and greater number of employees on more widely dispersed sites than the vast majority of managers in the private sector are expected to do (p.43).

However, we should not automatically dismiss experience from the world of commerce and industry, particularly as the exhortations Riley refers to have meant that the public services have already taken on management notions from these sources – for example performance review. Whilst these are being refined within commercial settings, their adaptation should not stagnate within the public sector.

In manufacturing industry, of course, supervision has been traditionally invariably understood to mean overseeing, looking at what is going on; an observation, rather than a conversation; 'walking the job' is often an important aspect of being a manager. Implicit in this understanding of supervision is the fact that the manager needs to know how the job is done, knows what to do when things go wrong and can advise on how the job might be done better. Equally importantly, the manager is observed whilst managing. The benefits of this are borne out by research findings on what is valued in a manager: Alimo-Metcalfe (1996) reviews recent research in the commercial world and notes that subordinates value quite different skills in their manager than do the managers' own seniors: 'Bosses tend to focus on technical managerial skills...subordinates appreciate and are more concerned with interpersonal skills, sensitivity, empowerment and visionary leadership' (p.27).

Most telling is the fact that, over time, subordinates' ratings of a manager's effectiveness are the more accurate predictor of ability: 'The major difference between the two groups is, of course, that subordinates are in an excellent position to observe managers frequently and in a wider range of situations than is their boss' (op.cit., p.27).

'Do as I do, not as I say' really is a powerful prescriptive and organisations ignore this saw at their own expense, as recent press coverage suggests:

> (A teacher) was escorted off school premises...pending a disciplinary hearing for 'serious misconduct'... This involved criticism of Ofsted in an internal handbook in the department of personal social education (PSE) 'Those who can't do, teach. Those who can't teach become PSE teachers and those who can't teach PSE become Ofsted inspectors' ...in an attempt to lighten up the 95-page manual.
> (*Guardian*, 7 January 1997)

Learning through observation is a valued aspect of much commercial management training, using the technology we associate more with the practice of family therapy. Consequently, chartered accountants are more likely to have watched themselves interviewing on video than have social services managers.

Thomas and Ely (1996) have researched the reasons why planned change within business organisations fails. They reiterate the need for organisations to create a 'collective responsibility' for change and that this is 'an attitude, a value'. They note that successful companies are those where managers have been given overlapping responsibilities. Of particular interest in the context of observation skills are their findings about what creates and fosters this approach. Some of them are surprisingly physical:

> In our study, departments with layouts that permitted people to see other's work had cycle times 4:4 faster than those with layouts that didn't... When people cannot see others at work misperceptions arise both about the nature of their jobs and about the pace, pressure and commitments of others. (p.79)

Within the private sector, performance review – the expectation that managers are assessed for their effectiveness and further development – has become received wisdom. Alimo-Metcalfe (1996) argues that feedback, properly understood, is 'essential for maintaining motivation and increasing effectiveness of performance'. However, 'the formalised process of providing it in the annual appraisal has generally proved to be a most disappointing ritual' (p.27).

This echoes Trowell and Miles' (1991) argument that, in social work practice, 'All too easily, observation can become a superficial, meaningless exercise... Imposition without observation is skewed at best, damaging at worst' (p.53).

Management theory advocates that effective feedback has two characteristics: it is *immediate* and it *operates at 360 degrees*. Immediacy seems self-explanatory: managers shouldn't confine feedback to a delayed, formal expression, say, at annual review.

However, it is worth looking at this notion in more detail. A family therapist or a social work practice teacher can give effective feedback because they are present to observe behaviour. A manager needs to have some equivalent processes. In other words, direct observation means they have to be there to see and to comment. Feedback of '360 degrees' means that managers expect feedback from those around them, from subordinates and peers as well as from their seniors. They will receive observations from some very different points of view.

Organisational Behaviour

Another source for the application of observation skills to social care management lies in the 'industrial observation' developed by Menzies-Lyth (1988) and, with particular regard to care organisations, by the work of the Tavistock Group (Obholzer and Roberts 1994).

It is against this background that management in social care agencies is encouraged to consider itself as open to scrutiny, to expect there to be connections between the nature of the work and their own behaviour and feelings. In this sense, management in social care may be quite different from management in the business and commercial fields. I shall return to this later.

Supervision

/This is undergoing something of a renaissance in social work. Until relatively recently, texts on supervision were not fashionable (Domini 1994). However, in the past few years interest has revived, stemming from a variety of sources, including the impetus of assessed practice models in NVQ development, growing interest in evidenced outcomes (Cheetham *et al.* 1992; Everitt and Hardiker 1996) and from applications of the concepts of reflective learning initiated by Schön (1987). |The organisational setting within which supervision takes place is understood, so that supervision is no longer a private activity nor is it focused solely on the professional development of the supervisee. Supervision is now expected to provide management information and act as a means to providing more effective services (Morrison 1994). The literature has also begun to consider the supervision needs of managers as well as of practitioners (Riley 1997). |

Supervision thinking is familiar with the concept of reflective processes, as expounded by Mattinson (1975), where the worker's behaviour and feelings can be useful pointers to what is happening in a client's life. Mattinson applies this to a wider stage and argues that the process is relevant throughout the organisation, where the relationships between clients and workers are repeated at all levels of organisational behaviour, building on Jacques' (1955) concept of institutional defences.

Management in Social Work and Social Care

Social work practice, social work teaching and business management and development can all make use of observation skills and their underlying concepts and values. Are they useful in social care management or is this too different from the worlds of practice and commerce?

There are real differences, and these need to be explicit if management in social care is to adapt some of this work successfully.

The Differences

There are differences between the private and public sectors, as Riley has noted above. The caring professions may well balk at the vocabulary of the business world and at their criteria for effectiveness and success. These should not be barriers to adapting useful notions. After all, systemic family therapy acknowledges its debts to engineering and biophysics when it uses feedback concepts.

However, there is a fundamental difference between managing in social care settings and in business that needs to be taken account of. This is that management and direct practice are both aspects of the same job, no matter how we try to divide them. The nature of the work has a direct effect upon how it is carried out. In this sense, a manager in retailing has a similar job to a manager in manufacturing, but a manager in social care works in an organisation where it is vital to recognise what Obholzer and Roberts (1994) describe as 'the fundamental dynamics arising from the nature of the work itself'.

Currently, there may be another significant difference between managers and practitioners in social work. Practitioners are increasingly used to observing and being observed as part of their initial and post-qualifying training. With this experience, they gain knowledge at a number of levels: they will develop their expertise in assessment, they will develop their epistemological understanding about the nature of knowledge and they will understand and be able to apply learning through observation throughout the range of professional activity. In contrast, their managers will have had very little opportunity to develop in these ways. Anxieties and resistance may be high.

The Similarities

More positively, managers and practitioners in social work share some skills too. The business sector recognises that a good manager needs inter-personal skills of a high order. What are these but part of the skilled social worker's repertoire? Parsloe (1996) highlights an equally vital shared skill when she describes her team's experience as University managers:

> Our backgrounds as social workers and social scientists stood us in good stead. We were all aware of the importance of process and were prepared to spend time on it…this is not universal and many people are extremely impatient of time spent on the process of decision making and cannot tolerate the confusion. They press for quick decisions and have no doubt that the decision is all that matters. (p.120)

This is where the fundamental characteristic of managing in social care becomes its strength. The nature of the work means that managers learn to operate in confusion and irresolvable difficulty (for a discussion of this theme see Darvill 1996).

Management and practice in social care have one significant similarity: much of the work is presumed to be done in private. Incidentally, this has probably never been the experience of front-line managers in residential and day care services where their behaviour is public and open to scrutiny by clients and staff but their experience has rarely been used as the organisational norm. However, no behaviour is really invisible, as Parsloe (1996) points out when she states that managers need 'to recognise the way in which their behaviour will, whether they like it or not, provide a model for practice' (p.116).

An Observation Framework for Managers in Social Work and Social Care

An observation framework for management seems the best way for pulling these experiences together. I suggest that applications of observation are fourfold and can be applied across the organisational hierarchy:

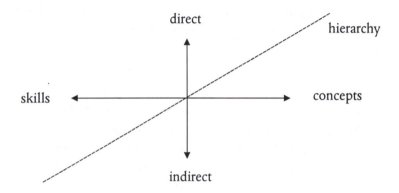

Direct Observation

Managers should expect to see and be seen and may have more opportunities for this than they realise. They see direct professional practice in a number of ways in their daily work as participant observers: when they walk through reception areas or attend case conferences or adoption and fostering panels, to name a few. As non-participant observers they could expand these contacts beyond what may be their usual timetable – how many managers, even at first-line level, spend time in duty rooms, waiting areas or interview rooms?

Similarly, the daily management timetable affords direct observation of management practice: the host of meetings that take up a manager's life at all levels in the organisation afford direct observation of management practice.

It is worth revisiting the difficulties noted by Trowell and Miles (1991), since managers are likely to face the same difficulties as child protection workers in establishing contracts: *what is the manager doing here?*; anxiety about their role: *what is the manager up to?*; and finding the content distressing: *how often do senior managers experience the emotional force of regular, direct contact with people in crisis and distress?*

When Mattinson and Sinclair (1979) undertook research in social service area offices they touched on how uncomfortable and useful an experience it was:

> We…experienced…the guilt induced by this spy role… In many ways our participant role gave us access to data which otherwise would have been denied us. In our contacts with the hierarchy we reacted with dismay to the way they appeared to perceive the situation of the social worker and we became trapped in a somewhat juvenile, even paranoid, stance as we urged our view upon them. (pp.19–20)

Underlying many of these difficulties is the power differential between manager and managed. Hierarchical structure cuts across professional status and autonomy and can divorce practice expertise from power. If the organisation is not clear about its primary functions, the manager's work will be different and more important than the practitioner's work. In these circumstances, observation by managers of those they manage will be experienced as oppressive, covert and antithetical to the professional task. Organisations could usefully ask themselves what conditions should prevail for formal observation to be an accepted aspect of development in the agency.

Managers are also observed directly by their peers and those they manage. I think that this phenomenon is what gives rise to the idea of 'the culture of the organisation', a limited notion since every organisation must be a 'United Nations' of cultures at any one time. Perhaps a more useful way of describing this is Mattinson's (1975) observation that 'Unconsciously we all mimic, probably more than we realise, continually picking up ways and attitudes from other people without giving them conscious thought' (p.43) as a way of understanding the effect of managers' behaviour on those who see them in action.

Observed behaviour will inevitably be a model to the viewer. The following example is illuminating:

> The deputy director of social services chaired an adoption panel. He was concerned that the social worker's presentation of the prospective adopters was focused only on their need to have a child. He explained his concerns to the social worker and suggested that he should meet

the couple with the social worker and explain the panel's decision not to approve them as potential adopters. After the interview the social worker said: 'I didn't know you could do that'.

This is learning on two levels: the manager took it to mean that the social worker had never seen him except behind a desk. It is also likely that the social worker had appreciated seeing an expert practitioner at work.

In some social service departments managers beyond front-line practice are encouraged to retain their ASW warrant. (The terms of the warrant require it to be used a number of times per year to be retained.) The joint benefits to managers of retaining an eye on practice and of their credibility in the eyes of their staff are many.

Indirect Observation

Much of the criticism of bureaucratised practice and management in social services concerns an emphasis on form rather than process. The notion of indirect observation could safeguard against overly-procedural thinking, as in the following example:

> Senior managers in a social work department became concerned when they noted that statistical returns from community care social workers showed 'no action' on a high proportion of allocated cases. Managers were unclear whether social workers were unco-operative about filling in statistics forms or whether they were accepting a lot of inappropriate referrals. On investigation, social workers explained that they hadn't 'done any work' on these cases. By this they meant that they hadn't accessed budgets for services. One case serves to illustrate the point: a GP referral asked for residential care for a recently bereaved elderly woman. The social worker visited over a number of weeks, talked with the widow about how she felt, involved her with the bereavement service, Cruse, and ascertained that the woman had told her GP how helpless she had felt at her husband's sudden death. At the end of the contact it was agreed that the widow did not want residential care, understood some of her grieving and had emotional support for this process.

Managers can interpret their data in several ways and if they consider only the parameters of procedural compliance, they will not understand what they see. If they observe the processes involved, this lets them look at the wider picture: what can they expect data to capture and what escapes? What covert message do staff receive when procedures do not reflect practice so that real work only happens when budgets are accessed?

Skills and Concepts

Any observation undertaken by managers needs a mandate, and this is where the skills and concepts of observation must be demonstrated. Observation is not a seek and destroy mission but has to be negotiated by permission, whatever the relative status in the department hierarchy of those involved. Feedback needs to be explicitly described – as different from comment, pejorative or otherwise. The manager, like the practitioner, needs to know how 'to distinguish between observation, hypothesis and assessment; the importance of not pre-judging situations; and the readiness to modify first impressions in the light of new information' (Wilson 1992, p.37).

Neutrality is also helpful in this context. It makes a virtue of the manager being 'out of touch' with practice and genuinely curious. The neutral stance required of the observer can give both managers and managed the opportunity to escape from the hierarchy imposed by departmental bureaucracy and can provide managers with what they often find lacking in their daily practice: the chance to step outside their administrative role, take time to reflect on what they see and begin to manage.

Feedback, then, is negotiated and accepted as an illumination of behaviour. It has to be evidenced and is open to debate. Its aim is to aid the positive change and problem solving that those being observed want to undertake. A recent annual performance review contained the chilling words: 'I know more about you than you realise'. This is not feedback, it is oppression!

Crossroad Benefits

Observation skills work in several directions: they can support the development of best practice but also management development in its own right. They can be used in all directions: up, down, across and from without the organisation. Mentoring and shadowing schemes give junior staff the opportunity to see senior managers at work and are usually understood to provide potential managers with early experience of the next stage of the job. These schemes are also an opportunity for managers to obtain some process observation from staff outside the immediate family – how often are junior staff asked to give their comments on the process of the senior management meeting they are allowed to observe?

Similarly, peer group managers could offer an 'outsider' observation to other parts of the department. This would be particularly useful now that departments can seem so intractably divided between purchasers and providers and echoes the findings of Thomas and Ely (1996) when they note the effect of managers with overlapping responsibilities – that is, the opportunity for contact and communication across otherwise closed groups.

Staff support groups that use an external observer to comment on their organisational dynamics in order to illuminate their work are relatively common in clinical and direct practice settings. They are fairly uncommon in the management levels of these agencies but would provide management supervision and development that was integral to the work of the organisation.

Knowing and Learning

I have commented briefly on how observation expertise can inform a worker's knowledge about how they learn and about the nature of knowledge. Le Riche and Tanner (1996) develop this epistemological framework with their 'narrative' model of observation. I will conclude with some questions about the consequences of applying this aspect of observation theory to the management of social care: what is the nature of knowledge, objectivity and evidence in the management context?

The debate about managing information (see NISW 1996 for an overview) argues for the transitions that need to be made from data to information, to knowledge and, finally, to decision making and action. The literature of expert knowledge in social care agencies discusses the subjectivity inherent in this process (for a wide-ranging exposition see Eraut 1994). This contrasts with stereotypical notions of management being about hard, 'scientific' data – which view of management, of course, maintains the divide between management and practice within social work agencies.

The way in which managers learn and make sense of what they see within an observation framework will reveal a number of processes in operation: they will have feelings; they will see what actually happens rather than what is expected or supposed to happen; they will distinguish between 'snapshot' observations and those repeated over time; and they will expect to analyse, communicate and test out their thinking. What does this mean in action?

Feelings

First, it acknowledges feelings as legitimate data. Child abuse inquiries are full of comment that workers and managers misunderstood risk because their emotional reactions to what they saw or heard about were not regarded as legitimate, that is objective, data.

What Actually Happens

How many managers, in their role as systems planners, actually undertake or view the undertaking of their procedures for themselves? (One wonders how many community care assessment forms would have hit the dust had managers tried operating them, in normal conditions, themselves.)

Evidencing Observations

This requires communication and discussion about what is seen and how it is understood. Departments as a whole will benefit from analysing their behaviour in terms of evidenced outcomes. They will expect to get the 360-degree picture from clients, carers, other agencies and their own hierarchies.

In short, managers, just as practitioners, will expect the narrative to be a necessary part of their understanding about the task in hand. This is the backdrop and defining force behind all their necessary technical skills, helping to focus all the work of the department on the primary task:

> Following their department's computerisation of records, a director and deputy director visited one of their area offices to view the new system in operation. They watched the file screen scroll past with all the boxes and headings filled in. The director turned to the deputy and said: 'But where's the story?'

In summary, then, I think observation can teach us a lot about working with other people to best effect – which is, after all, the definition of a manager. It offers us a bridge across the divide between management and practice in social care. It allows us to take useful learning from other management settings and integrate them within our own settings. Social care organisations that promote curiosity about their own behaviour and encourage this as a part of management practice and development will be the richer for it.

References

Alimo-Metcalfe, B. (1996) 'The feedback revolution.' *Health Services Journal,* 26–27, 13 June.

Barker, P. (1992) *Regeneration.* London: Penguin.

Burnham, J. and Harris, Q. (1988) 'Systemic family therapy: the Milan approach.' In E. Street and W. Dryden (eds) *Family Therapy in Britain.* Milton Keynes: OUP.

Cheetham, J., Fuller, R., McIvor, G. and Petch, A. (1992) *Evaluating Social Work Effectiveness.* Ballmoor: OUP.

Darvill, G. (1996) *Managing Contradiction and Avoidance – A Discussion Paper and Self-Audit.* London: NISW.

DoH (1988) *Protecting Children: A Guide for Social Workers Undertaking a Comprehensive Assessment.* London: HMSO.

Domini, L. (1994) *Management of Practice Expertise – A Literature Review.* London: NISW.

Eraut, M. (1994) *Developing Professional Knowledge and Competence.* London: Falmer Press.

Everitt, A. and Hardiker, P. (1996) *Evaluating for Good Practice.* Basingstoke: Macmillan.

Foucault, M. (1973) *The Birth of The Clinic: An Archaeology of Medical Perception.* London: Routledge.

HMSO (1995) *Child Protection: Messages from Research.* London: HMSO.

Jacques, E. (1955) 'Social systems as a defence against persecutory and depressive anxiety.' In M. Klein, P. Heimann and R.E. Money-Kyrle (eds) *New Directions in Psychoanalysis.* New York: Basic Books.

Le Riche, P. and Tanner, K. (1996) 'The way forward: developing an equality model of observation for social work practice and education.' *Issues in Social Work Education 16,* 2, 3–14.

Mattinson, J. (1975) *The Reflection Process in Casework Supervision.* London: Tavistock Institute of Medical Psychology.

Mattinson, J. and Sinclair, I. (1979) *Mate and Stalemate.* Oxford: Blackwell.

Menzies-Lyth, I. (1988) *Containing Anxiety in Institutions: Selected Essays, Vol 1.* London: Free Association Books.

Miller L., Rustin M., Rustin M. and Shuttleworth, J. (eds) (1989) *Closely Observed Infants.* London: Duckworth.

Morrison, T. (1994) *Staff Supervision in Social Care: An Action Learning Approach.* Harlow: Longman.

NISW (1996) *The Social Services Information Agenda Briefing No 17.* London: NISW.

Obholzer, A. and Roberts, V.Z. (eds) (1994) *The Unconscious at Work: Individual and Organisational Stress in the Human Services.* London: Routledge.

Parsloe, P. (1996) 'Managing for reflective learning.' In N. Gould and I. Taylor (eds) *Reflective Learning for Social Work.* Aldershot: Arena.

Parton, N. (1985) *The Politics of Child Abuse.* London: Macmillan.

Parton, N. (1996) 'Child protection, family support and social work: a critical appraisal of the department of health research studies in child protection.' *Child And Family Social Work 1,* 1, 3–11.

Pollit, C. (1993) *Managerialism and the Public Services.* Oxford: Blackwell.

Riley, P. (1997) 'Supervision of social service managers.' In J. Pritchard (ed) *Good Practice In Supervision: Statutory and Voluntary Agencies.* London: Jessica Kingsley Publishers.

Schön, D. (1987) *Educating the Reflective Practitioner: Toward a New Design for Teaching and Learning in the Professions.* San Francisco: Jossey Bass.

Tanner, K. and Le Riche, P. (1995) '"You see but you do not observe." The art of observation and its application to practice teaching.' *Issues in Social Work Education 15,* 2, 66–80.

Thomas, D. and Ely, R. (1996) 'Making differences matter: a new paradigm for managing diversity.' *Harvard Business Review,* Sept-Oct, 79–91.

Trowell, J. and Miles, G. (1991) 'The contribution of observation training to professional development in social work.' *Journal of Social Work Practice 5,* 1, 51–60.

Wilson, K. (1992) 'The place of child observation in social work training.' *Journal of Social Work Practice 6,* 1, 37–47.

CHAPTER EIGHT

The Observer as Participant

The Role of Observation in Systemic Couple and Family Therapy

Moira Doolan

When I am observing him, he actually observes my observing. We are both in an observing position... By observing his response to my observing, I can indirectly become an observer of my own observing. He observes in order to define who I am, in order for him to know how much he dares to engage in the conversation while conserving his integrity. He is making a picture of me, a moving picture and he gives that picture an explanation that tells him what he might expect from me. That explanation will guide his sayings and doings towards me in his relation to me. (Andersen 1990, p.35)

Observation is at the heart of systemic family therapy practice and training. Everything that has been written by systemic therapists is founded upon their observations of the individuals, couples and families they have seen in the course of their work. In therapy the context is change, and the therapist is in an active role, directing efforts toward some change. Thus in family therapy observation must always be considered as a process in which the observer is seen as actively taking in, making sense of what is being received and acting on what has been understood. There is no fundamental distinction between the therapist as observer and the therapist as commentator or intervener. At any given moment she may define what she is doing as just observing, or as actively intervening, but the distinction is arbitrary. Thus, in this chapter, whenever I talk about making observations I am also talking about the therapist taking part in whatever she is observing. Moreover, the observer in family therapy is also the observed. In current practice the therapist must seek to include herself in her own field of observation. It is also important to say that observing includes listening as well as seeing. Both behaviour and meaning are included in the field of observation, as well as the complex relationships between them.

In the introductory chapter Le Riche points to the complexity and multidimensionality of observation. Using her formulation, it can be said that observation in family therapy is systematic and intentional and draws on theoretical ideas generated by family therapists as well as other theories – for example attachment theory. At the same time, family therapists have recognised that what Le Riche terms 'the glance' may capture crucial information, in that it is accepted that theories are, by definition, constraining, and the therapist must seek to see and to receive that which may have been outside of her vision or understanding. In this chapter I will discuss how ideas in couple and family therapy about observation have evolved to include many of the issues identified in what Le Riche has termed 'scientific' and 'narrative' models of observation.

There are now many approaches to family and couple therapy and this chapter draws on those which are broadly called systemic. Direct observation has been part of the practice of systemic couple and family therapy from very early days, to the extent that family therapy was, quite literally, conceived in the process of observing interaction in families and trying to comprehend that interaction. Most of the early approaches to family therapy sought to effect change by intervening directly in these interactions. It therefore followed that planning for making interventions needed to happen while the therapy was taking place.

Thus in family and couple therapy observation is not an activity apart from the therapeutic work. It is common practice for teams or co-therapists to observe from behind a one-way screen, to communicate directly with the therapist about the process of the interview and devise interventions with the therapist. Direct observation is part of the therapy, and training therapists' observations of families and observation of training therapists working with families generally occur as part of this larger context. Experience has shown that observation cannot be regarded as neutral since the observer's theoretical base affects the process at every stage.

However, couple and family therapists also frequently work alone, without a team, and one of the goals of a training in systemic training is the development of an observing self, a capacity to see oneself as part of the process. This is a goal which can never be fully achieved, but, in constantly seeking to achieve it, a certain awareness of how the therapist as observer is constantly contributing to and being affected by the process is created. Crucial to this process is an awareness of the significance of gender, ethnicity, culture and other issues of power and difference.

In this chapter I will discuss systemic therapy and social work as separate entities, but this is a false dichotomy. Social workers have played a key role in the development of couple and family therapy as practitioners, trainers and writers. (For example, Burnham 1986; Draper, Gower and Huffington 1990; Satir 1964; Walters *et al.* 1988; Whiffen and Byng-Hall 1982.) Along with their colleagues in other helping professions, they have applied and developed their ideas in statutory, non-statutory and voluntary settings (Campbell and Draper 1985). In my view, all the observational processes which I will discuss in this chapter are directly applicable to the complex tasks of assessment and intervention which social workers undertake in their work with adults, children and families.

I will begin by outlining the early development of systemic family therapy. Some theoretical ideas in family therapy will be discussed in relation to what is observed, the way teams are organised in training situations and the position of the observer in relation to issues of power. Through use of a practice example I will discuss the process within the observing team in relation to the trainee therapist and the relationship between the therapist and family. In the final section I will discuss how ideas from observation in family therapy are of direct relevance to social work practice with children and families.

The Early Development of Systemic Family Therapy:
The Bateson Project

Gregory Bateson, an English anthropologist, attended a series of conferences held in New York in the 1940s sponsored by the Macy Foundation. The new science of cybernetics emerged from these conferences. Cybernetics concerns itself with the way non-living systems, such as the guidance mechanisms in rockets, regulate and control themselves.

Bateson also looked to the General Systems Theory developed by the biologist Von Bertalanffy. This theory proposed that living systems are characterised by the inflow and outflow of information that allows an organism simultaneously to maintain its integrity whilst adapting and changing in response to new circumstances. What interested him was how the different parts of the organism (system) interact together to make up the whole. In order to explain or describe the system under observation, one has to explain how its constituent parts are organised and interact. Bateson is largely credited with introducing and applying these ideas to the field of human communication and behaviour (Bateson 1972). One can see that these ideas from within the behavioural sciences shifted the unit of interest and observation away from the single, individual component part to the relationship between the part to the whole, between the individual and his context.

In 1952 Bateson established a research project on communication which laid the foundations from which family therapy developed and evolved. The project began by studying both human and animal communication in relation to the idea that, in communication, messages at one level are 'framed' or governed by messages at another level. They videotaped and analysed micro-sequences of interaction. Thus from the beginning, direct observation became integral to the process.

Bateson considered that there were different channels of communication: 'words, voice, body movement and context' (Haley 1976a, p.65). Problems in the form of paradoxes were thought to develop when there was discontinuity between levels, or between framing messages, and one form of these paradoxes was termed the double bind. Study of communication sequences between family members revealed that there was mutuality in these interactions and it was very difficult to know where to begin and end a sequence. This led to a dissatisfaction with the idea of one person as 'victim' and a search for a model which considered the whole family. Drawing on systems theory, family interaction was depicted 'as a closed information system in which variations in output or behaviour are fed back in order to correct the systems' responses' (Haley 1976a, p.65). Thus it was suggested that family members control the range of communication/behaviour in the family through a circular process of interaction in which each influences and is influenced by the other.

This systems view of communication and behaviour in families was shared by all participants in the project, but there were also significant differences. One group, which Haley terms the 'behavioural' wing, thought that the focus should be on observations which could be 'observed and verified', while the 'higher generalisation' wing thought that it was also important to include emotional experience and how things are perceived (Haley 1976a, p.74). These differences have been maintained and developed in the theory and practice of family therapy, although not necessarily in opposition to one another. It might be said that the Strategic, Structural and Brief Therapy approaches represent the behavioural wing in that their focus of observation and change is the direct interactions between people, while the Milan, Narrative and Brief Solution Focused Approaches represent the higher generalisation wing in that they also focus on beliefs and meanings.

The dominant idea of the systemic/communications-based family therapy developed by the early pioneers of systemic family therapy was that problems arise and are maintained in the recursive interactions and communications between family members. It followed that the therapy they developed first of all demanded direct observation of those interactions and that the therapist would intervene directly in those interactions. I would suggest that this remains true across the spectrum of systemic therapies.

Within the behavioural wing, early family therapists saw themselves as scientists who were apart from the family systems they observed. From their observations they identified certain patterns which I will discuss in more detail below. Fields such as developmental psychology, which study the factors in child abuse and neglect (for example, Cicchetti 1989), have also adopted process models which consider these factors at a micro-interactional level. Thus for family therapists and social workers alike it is important to have both skills in observing micro-interactional processes and an openness to an expanding knowledge base from research in a number of fields which identify processes which need to be attended to in order to understand problems and successes in families. These directly observed processes of interaction come into what Le Riche has described as the scientific end of the observation continuum. Let us look at this approach more closely.

Observation of Family Interaction:
Communication, Structure and Emotion

Strategic, Structural and Brief therapists including Haley (1976b), Minuchin (1979) and Watzlawick, Bavelas and Jackson (1967) have contributed crucial ideas to our understanding of what it is important to observe in family process. One of the cornerstone ideas developed from the Bateson project is that communication has both an information-giving or *content* function and a *process* or relationship-defining function. For example, a husband who says 'where is my shirt' is not just asking for information, he is conveying the expectation that his wife has responsibility for taking care of his physical needs.

Communication is also described as digital and analogic (Watzlawick *et al.* 1967). Digital communication essentially refers to the use of language, which is, by definition, limited because it is arbitrarily giving a name to something. Analogic communication includes all non-verbal communication, such as body language and the emotional tone of the communications which may have a more direct relationship to that which is being named. It is connected to symbolic logic and, in language, to the use of metaphor. Family therapists are interested in the ambiguities or conflicts between these different aspects of communication and the behavioural or pragmatic effect of communications. A classic example in child protection of the significance of observing these different aspects of communication would be a mother who gives a plausible explanation of a suspected non-accidental injury while, at the same time, it was observed that the child was anxious, watchful and apparently gearing his behaviour to subtle cues from her.

Family therapists have observed that interactions are frequently recursive – that is, they are circular and self-maintaining. They are interested in the patterns formed in relationships. For example, an argument in which all participants are exchanging angry insults, leading to more angry insults, would be called symmetrical, as would an affectionate exchange of appreciative comments.

Attention is also paid to the hierarchical and executive organisation of the family, particularly in regard to generational relationships. If there is an alliance between a grandfather and child in opposition to the father in relation to disciplinary issues, this might be destructive and confusing for the child.

Emotional relationships are conceived in terms of distance and intensity. Attention is paid to the emotional boundaries, ranging from those which are too *rigid*, resulting in insensitivity to needs for nurturance and affection, to those which are too *diffuse* or indistinct, resulting in an emotional over-involvement which erodes a sense of personal autonomy.

Family systems therapists are also interested in the temporal aspect of presentation of problems and times of transition are seen as being particularly significant, whether developmental or caused by some unexpected crisis. The concept of the family life cycle, of families moving through developmental stages, is very important (Carter and McGoldrick 1988).

Thus, in summary, at a 'behavioural' level a family therapist would observe the nature of the communication, the hierarchical and emotional organisation of the family and the nature of the self-reinforcing and maintaining repetitive interactional sequences.

Observation of Family Interaction:
Family Beliefs and Meaning Systems

The Milan associates, and Feminist and Narrative therapists referred to in this section, could be said to represent the 'higher generalisation wing' in family therapy. I will describe how the views of many family therapists about observation now correspond very closely to what Le Riche has termed the narrative aspects of observation.

Some of the early family therapists, including Murray Bowen, were interested in extended family networks and how themes and issues could be played out across generations. Thus it might be said that as well as finding ways to map the family system in terms of its communications and hierarchical and emotional relationships, family therapists were also trying to map the meaning system of the family.

The Milan associates and others began to apply their systemic analyses beyond the family itself to professional systems (Palazzoli *et al.* 1980). They observed the process between themselves and family members in the same terms as interactions between family members. For example, an observing team (or the therapist herself) might notice that in an effort to offer a more positive understanding of a child's behaviour, the therapist had instead engaged in an escalating battle with the parents with the effect that no progress was being made. The definition of what constituted 'the system' became much less tied to the nuclear family and much more to what system was *meaningful* for the family in relation to the problem.

A major shift in thinking occurred when it was suggested that 'the family' was not an entity that could be observed apart from its context. Another view of cybernetics, termed 'second order cybernetics', was proposed, which views living systems as being open and constantly changing through inevitable interactions. A key influence in bringing about this 'second order cybernetics' perspective has been Social Constructivism, which takes the view that there is no objective reality.

Family therapists became interested in observing the differences in perceptions between family members, how those differences are expressed, and how those differences might fit or not fit. They continued to observe and track interactional sequences around the problem presented by the family, but they also developed interviewing techniques aimed at 'observing' or identifying how different members of the family 'saw' and understood these interactions (Palazzoli *et al.* 1980).

From this perspective, the therapist can no longer be regarded as an observer who stands outside a closed system. Instead, by definition, the therapist and the family create a new system in which the therapist must regard herself as part of the system to be observed (Dell 1985). From this perspective, the therapist cannot be seen as neutral or objective and, therefore, she must be constantly considering how her ideas and theories are constructing what she is observing.

A further shift in thinking about what needed to be brought into the range of observation occurred when feminists began to challenge family therapists about failing to take account of abuses of power, such as men's violence against women and sexual abuse of children. They argued that recognising that there are mutual effects in interaction does not necessarily mean that these effects are equal. For example, a child who is behaving defiantly contributes to the development of an escalating control battle with his father, but they are not equally responsible, nor do they have equal resources to alter this pattern (MacKinnon and Miller 1987). Feminists also pointed to the failure to take account of the impact of institutionalised differences of power, such as those between women and men, black and white people, and homosexual, lesbian and heterosexual people, and how these societal beliefs and norms affected the everyday transactions in families (MacLeod and Saraga 1988; Goldner 1985).

An equally fruitful approach to power in relation to family therapy has come via ideas of Social Constructionism, which argues that all knowledge is created in discourse – that is, in interaction with others. As certain discourses become institutionalised, those discourses, and the practices supported by those discourses, are given warrant, or power, over other discourses.

Drawing on the work of Foucault, Narrative therapists White and Epston (1989) are among those who have brought a new discourse on power into family therapy. Within this way of thinking, all language, verbal or non-verbal, is generative and has meaning. Certain ideas or knowledge, whether of individuals or groups within society, can become subjugated while others become dominant. Within this frame, the therapist must begin by observing herself. What are her own beliefs? What authority does she have in relation to gender, ethnicity, class, professional status or sexuality? In an interview with a family, with whom does she speak, what questions does she ask? If she intervenes or takes action, what warrant does she use to do that and what is the effect of that action on others? What beliefs guide her to ask or not ask questions of particular people?

The stance of the therapist is to be active in helping people to create new discourses or draw on alternative discourses which are less oppressive. The therapist will be interested in what discourses are dominant within the family and how individuals, or the family as a whole, may be oppressed by certain ideas and practices – for example in relation to gender and ethnicity. She will seek to help them bring forward ways of thinking and behaving which are more satisfying to them and, in this endeavour, she may call upon a whole range of people who are identified by the family as significant. In helping the family members to create new narratives she will have to seek alternative stories which the family already have, an observational process which is as exacting as any other (Boyd-Franklin 1989; Goldner *et al.* 1990; White and Epston 1989).

Within this frame, the therapist will always be aware that she has power but will be trying to employ it to empower others. She will actively consult her clients about their view of her actions. She will continuously observe her own actions in relation to how she may be maintaining problems in people's lives. When working with families who are culturally or ethnically different, she may seek consultation from colleagues or community groups about her practices (McLean 1994).

Thus, in current practice, the role of systemic therapist as observer is a very complex one, and similar issues apply to social workers in practice and training. It is impossible to observe without having a theory about what is being observed, and that theory shapes what we see. There is now a professional knowledge base which it is important to draw upon in making observations. However, neither observations nor practices based on professional knowledge bases are neutral or value-free. Within a narrative frame, the therapist must be aware of the constitutive nature of her observations and practices while, at the same time, seeking to understand and bring forward the ideas and beliefs of her clients.

Observation and Training in Systemic Family and Couple Therapy and Applications to Social Work

In Britain, training in systemic couple and family therapy normally includes two years of pre-clinical training in which trainees are introduced to the models of therapy and begin to apply these ideas to their current working practice. At this level of training, extensive use is made of experiential exercises to develop skills in observation. Trainees are asked to move between participant and observer, focusing on the same interactive patterns which they will identify and respond to in therapy, and practising interviewing skills and interventions (Draper *et al.* 1990). In such exercises the role of observer is as a commentator. This process of moving between participating and reflecting is directed toward developing the capacity for self-observation and reflexivity as well as learning specific techniques of assessment and intervention.

The one-way mirror and videotape are commonly used direct observational methods in systemic approaches to therapy. At a pre-clinical level trainees may observe sessions of work by experienced family therapists which are designed as seminars to introduce them to ideas and practices in family therapy. At this stage, extensive use is also made of reviews of videotapes of work by family therapists.

All family therapists trained in the United Kingdom who are eligible to register as psychotherapists must have 320 hours of directly supervised clinical practice, as part of a team, using a one-way mirror. Trainees in family therapy move back and forth between sessions where they may be an observer, to sessions where they are being observed, to observing themselves on videotape. There is a continuous process of taking in, reflecting, acting, taking in and reflecting.

Most teams using the one-way mirror meet prior to seeing the family or couple to orient themselves in a way which is appropriate to their way of working. During the session the supervisor may be in direct contact with the therapist through the use of the ear bug, telephone or by knocking on the door. Many teams break for discussion during the interview to form an intervention, which frequently takes the form of a message to the family, or messages may be delivered directly to the family by the team. A post-discussion follows, which formulates ideas for the next session.

How direct observational methods are used tends to be isomorphic with the theoretical approach, in training as well as in therapy. It follows that there is enormous diversity in the way that teams are organised to work together behind the screen and I am only able to discuss these differences here in broad brush strokes. Two key factors are the theoretical approach and observational skills which the trainee is learning and their stage of development in training. As Mazza (1985) states: 'Training therapists in a directive therapy requires a directive training, in which therapists learn by doing' (p.94). It thus follows that if the trainee is learning about what we earlier called the 'behavioural' aspects of systemic therapy by observing from behind the screen, supervisors will 'teach' them directly about what they are observing and how they may intervene. Similarly, supervisors will instruct trainee therapists about what to do when they are with families. This directive approach is in keeping with the therapeutic approach of bringing about change through directly intervening in the interactional patterns of the family.

Where the emphasis is on meaning which is created through context, and, therefore, the observer must be included in observations, the emphasis may be on the interactions between the therapist and family members as much as between the family members themselves. In this case the supervisor would rarely contact the therapist during the interview. This is in keeping with the idea that there is no one 'right' hypothesis about what is happening and trainees are encouraged to follow their own ideas once in the interview with the family. If there is an inter-session break when there is an exchange of ideas between the therapist and the therapy team, the observing trainees' contributions are equally as valid as the contributions made by other members of the team. The emphasis is on learning a way of thinking through being directly involved in, and reflecting on, the process of therapy itself (Pirotta and Cecchin 1985).

If trainees are learning to map the belief system of the family around the problem, with particular regard to how the ideas of different members fit or don't fit together, trainees might be asked to try to track the recurrent themes in the interview. For example, the team might observe that each time a couple begin to talk intimately, an argument develops, and that they have both told stories about intimacy being frightening or dangerous.

Andersen and his team have evolved a particular method for using the team behind the screen, which has been given the name 'the reflecting team'. Instead of the therapist joining the team behind the screen for a consultation, the therapist and family go behind the screen and observe the team making reflections on what they have observed, or, if the screen is not available, the team sit in the room with the therapist and family. Reflections are not made with the intention of having a particular effect but rather are offered as ideas which may or may not be useful to the family members or to the therapist. This is in keeping with the idea that reality is constructed and that each person constructs their own view. Reflections are invited from the family members on what they have heard, to which the therapist can respond (Andersen 1987).

Current practice in training family therapists recognises the constitutive nature of the power relationship between supervisor and trainee. In directly observing a trainee's work, the emphasis would be on helping the trainee use prior experience to develop the ideas and techniques as part of the learning process. The supervisor offers ideas rather than instruction. Following an interview, the supervisor, or a reflecting team, interviews the therapist about how they were able to achieve certain outcomes which promoted change with the family in the interview. Other experiential exercises are also used to help the therapist develop an appreciation of her unique abilities. In this way the personal agency of the therapist is being promoted. The therapist is not invited to scrutinise herself but to notice when she is instrumental in moments of change, thus learning by her own experience how to help clients learn to observe themselves in this way (White 1992).

To my mind, the above ideas can usefully be incorporated within basic and post-qualifying training of social workers specialising in work with children and families and child protection. Children and families social workers undertake complex assessments of risk and need in a climate of diminishing resources. The ability to observe and understand issues of family structure, patterns of interaction and the impact of belief systems is central to the assessment process. It is this information which informs and guides subsequent intervention. A current example of this in social work practice would be the use of observation in enabling social workers to make accurate assessments of emotional abuse in families, paying attention not only to 'abusive events' but also to the underlying processes (DoH 1995). Direct observational methods can also assist the trainee in becoming what family therapists would term self-reflexive – that is, able to observe how their actions directly affect the course of the interview and to reflect on what guides them to respond or act in a particular way.

In the practice example which follows I will attempt to demonstrate the use of observation across the spectrum of ideas which I have discussed. The example which I am using will be familiar to social workers in a range of practice settings and the therapist in this example is a social worker in a child guidance setting.

The Use of Observation: A Practice Example

A family are attending their first session at their local child guidance clinic. The father had referred himself to social services because he was afraid that he might hit his six-year-old son, who he described as being beyond his control. The duty social worker was very impressed with his high level of motivation and thought that it would be inappropriate to respond using child protection procedures. She had arranged for him to be seen at child guidance. The father is black British and the mother is white British.

The female black trainee family therapist who is seeing them initially felt anxious and exposed while being observed but she and her supervisor, who is a white Irish man, have developed a good rapport. She now feels supported by him and the other members of the observing team. The excerpt below occurs midway through the session.

Both the team and the therapist observe the son attempting for the third time in as many minutes to climb onto a window ledge from a chair. His father shouts in an angry voice: 'Get down you little sod, how many times do I have to tell you! Once more and you will get a smack'. The child gets down, but gets up a minute later and climbs up again. The father looks accusingly at the mother, then hunches over in his chair and looks down. The mother turns to the therapist and says wearily: 'you see, he is impossible. He never listens no matter what we do'.

The therapist thinks to herself that in this situation the father's anger, and the child's failure to comply, maintain one another in a symmetrical battle and that the mother is involved in reducing the emotional intensity.

Comment: The therapist begins by observing the relationship patterns which operate around the problem.

The therapist notes the lack of congruity between the severity of the father's words and tone of voice, and his lack of action, and she wonders whether there are higher levels of belief operating to constrain the father.

Comment: The therapist begins to explore the possibility that in this case the problem may be maintained by beliefs as well as by the recursive pattern itself.

The therapist thinks that in turning to her, the mother is indicating her sense of helplessness in the situation, while the child is perceived by both parents as having a lot of control. She also notes the parents' emotional tone, their sense of shame and despair, and the child's bewilderment and unhappiness. She notices that they are evoking her compassion.

Comment: The therapist includes herself in the interaction pattern to be observed, including her emotional response.

The therapist says: 'It sounds as though you have tried many ways to sort things out already. It would really help me to understand if you could tell me what you've done so far'.

Behind the screen a second trainee therapist, a white British woman, notes how gently and warmly the therapist has spoken to the parents and that they both appear to relax a little. She makes a note to feed this back to the therapist at the end of the session.

Comment: The team member observes the process of the interaction between the therapist and the family and plans to use it to help her colleague recognise her strengths as a developing therapist.

The supervisor comments to the other team members that the therapist appears to have recognised that there is an invitation from the family for her to take charge of the situation but, at the same time, she must take care not to take charge of the child directly or she will further undermine their confidence and self-esteem. In inviting the parents to help her, she is recognising their expertise.

Comment: For the benefit of the second trainee, the supervisor draws attention to the dilemma the therapist is placed in, and her skill in empowering the parents through helping them recognise their own expertise.

As the parents describe how they have tried to solve the difficulty, the therapist thinks the parents were defining the behaviour in the room as an example of the problems for which they are seeking help and, therefore, as an opening for her to respond to in trying to help them.

Comment: The therapist observes the parents' behaviour in relation to herself and understands their behaviour as information about what they are wanting help with.

Behind the screen another member of the team, an Indian man, a psychologist in the team, comments that the parents and child are feeling very defeated by the cycle they are caught in and wonders if using the Narrative therapy technique of externalising defeat would be useful to the family.

Comment: The team member is beginning to gather ideas which may be useful to the therapist and the family in the reflecting team's comments.

The therapist asks questions about the parents' work situations because she has had hints that they both feel more competent in that arena. She learns that the father is very competent at his job. He says it is very important to him that he is in control and he feels utterly frustrated that he cannot manage his son. He explains that his father did not live with the family from the time he was three and he feels ill-equipped to be a father. His says his mother found it hard to manage but somehow 'kept going'. Suddenly he relaxes and starts to tease his partner about being the boss at work and the boss at home, so how can one small boy give her so much trouble?

The therapist notices that the mother has listened very attentively to him and that as he finishes speaking, she reaches over and squeezes his hand. He smiles at her and then says to the therapist: 'she has had a tough time too'. The therapist notes the consistency between the warmth of the emotional tone and what the parents are saying to one another. She thinks that they probably work quite well together and feels hopeful that she can help them work together to manage their son. She is increasingly convinced that it is beliefs connected to their childhood experiences which are impeding them in being effective in managing their child.

Comment: The therapist is using information from both analogic and digital communication to build a picture of the effectiveness of the parent's relationship.

The mother explains that her father was very strict: 'He left my mother to do everything, but felt he could interfere whenever he wanted'. She smiles at her partner and says: 'I don't understand why our son doesn't do what [his father] asks him to do. If my father had been as kind to me as he is to him, I would have done anything he asked'. Her partner beams with pleasure at this praise.

The therapist notices the little boy smile as he sees his father smile, and he crawls onto his father's lap for a cuddle. The therapist decides that it is time to begin to make an intervention and decides to externalise the problem – a technique from Narrative Therapy.

She says: 'I am really impressed by you both in so many ways. You have both come through tough times as children and doubt seems to have come into both of your lives and made you feel that you couldn't make a good job of being parents. I've noticed you are already well on the road but doubt stops you from seeing that. For a start, you both have so far refused to hit your son, even when doubt has tricked you into thinking you don't know what else to do. You've been prepared to feel ashamed and humiliated rather than hit him. You've said you play with him, give him lots of affection, and we know that those are the things which really help children want to work with parents'.

The observing team note that both parents are now sitting up in their chairs and have moved closer to each other. They are both smiling as she speaks.

The therapist says: 'I'll bet there are times already when you are successful in getting [your son] to do what you want'. She asks them if they can identify times when they have felt they managed their son as they would have wished. At first neither of them can think of any occasions, but each is then able to think of an example of when the other managed well.

Comment: The therapist has made an intervention which bears out her earlier observation that the parents are generally resourceful and work well together.

The father then goes on to say: 'it's a matter of pride, if you know what I mean'.

The therapist understands this to be a reference to racist stereotypes about black fathers being absent or aggressive, or both. This is an issue about which she personally feels very deeply because her own father was gentle and supportive, as her brothers are now with their families, and she knows how oppressed they have felt because often they have to work to be recognised for who they are.

She spends some time helping the father to define ways in which he has defeated racism and been the kind of father he wants to be.

Comment: The therapist is aware of her own personal feelings and is able to use them as a resource in this situation to assist the father.

Behind the screen her Indian colleague notes that she is doing a great job with the father but the mother and child are looking decidedly left out. The supervisor thanks him for his comments and wonders to himself if he has been afraid to name this issue to himself because he is white.

He phones into the therapist and comments that they are full of admiration for the great job she has done in helping the father and wonders if she could enlist the father's help in working with the mother to identify ways in which she succeeds in being the mother she would like to be. The therapist smiles in acknowledgement and begins to work with the mother.

Comment: The supervisor is able to draw on his colleague's comments and his own capacity to be self-reflexive to assist the therapist in her work with the family.

Shortly after, the observing team exchange places with the therapist and family to form a reflecting team. The white trainee therapist starts off by saying she thinks that the little boy is very fortunate to have parents who are so courageous and who have so much commitment to giving him the loving home that they didn't have themselves. She says that they are also doing this for each other and already they have succeeded in creating something very different than they had. The psychologist says that he noticed in the session that there were occasions when both parents had succeeded in getting the little boy to comply and he describes these in detail. Behind the screen the mother smiles and says softly: 'I've never thought of it that way before'. The supervisor has been very moved by the father's courage and wants to support him. He fears that he may sound patronising but decides to risk it and says: 'as an Irish man I know something about prejudice, but as a white man I know I can never fully appreciate just how much racism can undermine people. I just want to say I admire you Mr...for the way you are standing against all that and offering your son something different'.

Comment: The reflecting team use their 'warrant' as members of the team to try to help the parents become more aware of their considerable abilities as parents and thus empower them in relation to managing their son. They also support them in recognising the direct impact racism has on their lives and relationships.

After the family leave, the observing team make comments to the therapist about her work with the family to assist her in recognising her strengths and abilities.

In this example I have tried to show how the therapist and observing team can work together, on the basis of their direct observations, to help the family. I have tried to show that it is both possible and necessary to integrate observations on a number of levels to address the complexity of issues which social workers commonly meet in their practice.

The Department of Health (1995) publication *Child Protection: Messages from Research* pointed to the need to move away from child protection procedures as the main form of intervention to paying attention to 'the way parents generally deal with their children and to the usual temperature of family life' (p.67). The example I have used here illustrates that responding effectively to threats or actual physical and emotional abuse, like sexual abuse, requires a sensitive and informed intervention. In the final section I will discuss how some of these ideas can be further applied to social work practice.

Relevance to Social Work Practice

Social workers are asked to assess and intervene in complex human problems across the life span. They need conceptual frameworks which inform them in knowing how and what to observe in their direct encounters with families and how to connect those observations to generational issues, genetic and social factors and wider systems. Systemic therapy provides a framework which enables social workers to connect observations at a number of levels to make effective assessments and interventions when combined with the now considerable literature on child abuse and neglect. It is in observing micro-interactional processes in detail that a social worker will gain understanding of the attachment relationships, the emotional climate, the hierarchical structure, the level of coerciveness, the belief systems, the management strategies and problem-solving abilities of a family – all of which are crucial to making assessments in child care and mental health. (See Reder and Lucey 1995 for comprehensive examples of how systemic ideas can be applied in assessment of parenting.)

Like family therapists, social workers need to be aware of how context influences what they perceive and how they themselves will be perceived. The belief systems of the agency, and the worker, will affect the process as much as the family's beliefs and behaviour. In social constructionist terms, social workers are viewed as having a very powerful warrant because they have the power to instigate procedures which can result in children being removed from home or, in adult mental health, of people being hospitalised. Clients' responses will also depend on their perceptions and views of the social worker's ethnicity, culture, gender and so on. Using a social constructionist frame, a social worker should be aware that in making an assessment, they need to gain an understanding of how they are perceived, since that affects what the client is willing to reveal and how they will behave.

Reder, Duncan and Gray (1993), in their analysis of child abuse enquiries, provide clear evidence for observing the pattern which develops between the social worker and the family. For example, they identified a pattern which they termed 'closure' where families default appointments, which leads to a pattern of increased but *unsuccessful* attempts on the part of the social worker to gain entry. In this situation the social worker could become frustrated and 'forget' the family. Being aware that such a pattern could indicate an increased risk of abuse helps the social worker to decide how to intervene.

Another important aspect of observing the worker/family system is to remember that a new system is created when the worker is in interaction with the family. The support, or presence, of the social worker may give an enhanced picture of how the family is coping, which could, in turn, give the social worker a distorted view of the level of risk in a family. Equally, where a family has been receiving help for some time, the social worker may make an assessment which indicates that the family is less competent than they are, or would be without the social worker's involvement.

Family therapists have also pointed to the importance of processes within and between agencies in relation to decision making. Firmly held beliefs may exclude important information being considered and issues of whose views are given weight are also relevant. More junior members of staff may have more direct contact with families but not be listened to as much as those with greater status.

Conclusion

In this chapter I have shown how observation is intrinsic to training and practice in systemic couple and family therapy. I have suggested that all the methods described – for example direct observation of work by experienced practitioners with families 'live' or on video, supervision of the trainee's own work 'live' or on video and experiential exercises which develop skills in observation – are applicable to social work training. I have argued that much of what is considered important for family therapists is equally relevant to social workers, including the capacity to observe interactional processes, an appreciation of how the observer affects the process, an understanding of belief systems, a knowledge of wider systems and how cultural and societal issues are reflected in moment-by-moment interactions.

There are crucial implications here for both social work training and practice, at a time when the social work role is increasingly formulated in terms of care planning without apparently recognising the level of sophistication which is necessary to make effective assessments. Too often in the past, child abuse inquiries have revealed that social workers had been inadequately prepared for the tremendously difficult tasks they undertake on a daily basis. Guidelines, such as *Protecting Children: A Guide for Social Workers Undertaking a Comprehensive Assessment* (DoH 1988), are important markers for practice but social workers require training of the depth and complexity I have described here to enable them to meet the grave responsibilities we place on them to protect and assist the most vulnerable members of our society.

References

Andersen, T. (1987) 'The reflecting team.' *Family Process 26*, 415–428.

Andersen, T. (1990) *The Reflecting Team: Dialogues and Dialogues about the Dialogues.* Broadstairs: Borgmann.

Bateson, G. (1972) *Steps to an Ecology of Mind.* Northvale: Jason Aranson Inc.

Boyd-Franklin, N. (1989) *Black Families in Therapy.* New York: Guilford Press.

Burnham, J. (1986) *Family Therapy.* London: Tavistock Publications.

Campbell, D. and Draper, R. (eds) (1985) *Applications of Systemic Family Therapy: the Milan Approach.* London: Academic press.

Carter, E. and McGoldrick, M. (eds) (1988) *The Changing Family Life Cycle: A Framework for Family Therapy.* (2nd edn.). New York: Allyn and Bacon.

Cicchetti, D. (1989) 'How research on child maltreatment has informed the study of child development: perspectives from developmental psychopathology.' In D. Cicchetti and V. Carlson (eds) *Child Maltreatment: Theory and Research on the Causes and Consequences of Child Abuse and Neglect.* Cambridge: Cambridge University Press.

Dell, P. (1985) 'Understanding Bateson and Maturana.' *Journal of Marital and Family Therapy 11*, 1, 1–20.

DoH (1988) *Protecting Children: A Guide for Social Workers Undertaking a Comprehensive Assignment.* London: HMSO.

DoH (1995) *Child Protection: Messages from Research.* London: HMSO.

Draper, R., Gower, M. and Huffington, C. (1990) *Teaching Family Therapy.* London: Karnac Books.

Goldner, V. (1985) 'Feminism and family therapy.' *Family Process 24*, 31–47.

Goldner, V., Penn, P., Sheinberg, M. and Walker, G. (1990) 'Love and violence: gender paradoxes in volatile attachments.' *Family Process 29*, 343–364.

Haley, J. (1976a) 'Development of a theory: a history of a research project.' In C. Sluzki and D. Ransom (eds) *Double Bind: The Foundation of the Communicational Approach to the Family.* New York: Grune and Stratton.

Haley, J. (1976b) *Problem Solving Therapy.* San Francisco: Jossey Bass.

MacLeod, M. and Saraga, E. (1988) 'Challenging the orthodoxy: towards a feminist theory.' *Feminist Review: Family Secrets. Child Sexual Abuse 28*, Spring, 16–55.

MacKinnon, L. and Miller, D. (1987) 'The new epistemology and the Milan approach: feminist and sociopolitical considerations.' *Journal of Marital and Family Therapy 13*, 2, 138–155.

Mazza, J. (1985) 'Training strategic therapists: the use of indirect techniques.' In H. Liddle, D. Breunlin and R. Schwartz (eds) *Handbook of Family Therapy Training and Supervision.* New York: Guilford Press.

McLean, C. (1994) 'A conversation about accountability with Michael White.' *Dulwich Centre Newsletter,* 2&3, 68–79.

Minuchin, S. (1974) *Families and Family Therapy.* London: Tavistock Publications.

Palazzoli, M.S., Boscolo, L., Cecchin, G. and Prata, G. (1980) 'Hypothesizing-circularity-neutrality: three guidelines for the conductor of the session.' *Family Process* 19, 3–12.

Pirrotta, S. and Cecchin, G. (1985) 'The Milan training program.' In H. Liddle, D. Breunlin and R. Schwartz (eds) *Handbook of Family Therapy Training and Supervision.* New York: Guilford Press.

Reder, P., Duncan, S. and Gray, M. (1993) *Beyond Blame: Child Abuse Tragedies Revisited.* London: Routledge.

Reder, P. and Lucey, C. (eds) (1995) *Assessment of Parenting: Psychiatric and Psychological Contributions.* London: Routledge.

Satir, V. (1964) *Conjoint Family Therapy.* Palo Alto, CA: Science and Behaviour Books.

Walters, M., Carter, B., Papp, P. and Silverstein, O. (1988) *The Invisible Web: Gender Patterns in Family Relationships.* New York: Guilford Press.

Watzlawick, P., Bavelas, J. and Jackson, D. (1967) *Pragmatics of Human Communication.* New York: W.W. Norton and Co.

Whiffen, R. and Byng-Hall, J. (1982) (eds) *Family Therapy Supervision: Recent Developments in Practice.* London: Academic Press.

White, M. (1992) 'Family therapy training and supervision in a world of experience and narrative.' In D. Epston and M. White (eds) *Experience, Contradiction, Narrative and Imagination: Selected Papers of David Epston and Michael White 1989–1991.* Adelaide: Dulwich Centre Publications.

White, M. and Epston, D. (1989) *Narrative Means to Therapeutic Ends.* New York: W.W. Norton and company

Acknowledgements

I wish to acknowledge the generous contribution made by Phil Roberts in the initial planning and writing of this chapter.

Conclusion

Pat Le Riche

The Scope of the Book

The aim of this book has been to illuminate two major aspects of the complex and diverse concept of observation in social work. The first aim was to develop the concept by incorporating a power perspective into observation, therefore enabling existing approaches to be extended to include the dimensions of equality and oppression. The second aim was to widen the scope of ideas about observation from the context of work with children and families, where they had been almost exclusively located, and apply them to a range of different groups, agencies and contexts. In this last section of the book I will draw together some of the main themes and discuss the emerging issues which have been presented before going on to look at some possibilities for the future continuation of the journey we have been describing.

The Application of Observation

One of the major routes that has been charted is the progress of the use of observation in social work from its starting point in psychoanalytic theory to later applications which offered practical understanding of the development of young children (Miles and Bridge 1997; Rustin 1989; Trowell and Miles 1991). We have described earlier how high levels of anxiety about the quality of social work practice with children and their families led to attempts to incorporate knowledge from psychoanalytic settings (particularly the Tavistock Clinic in London) to basic DipSW training. At that stage, observation was regarded mainly as a useful tool in assessment, particularly in relation to child protection (DoH 1988). From a different theoretical approach and set of preoccupations, ideas about the assessment of competence took up and incorporated observational skills in both education and practice. In social work education observation became part of the repertoire of learning and assessment in work with adults as a hierarchy of observation was developed at basic and post-qualifying levels in the practice curriculum (Tanner and Le Riche 1995). Currently, observation has a more central position in social work education than it does in social work practice and this applies both to courses at the basic and post-qualifying levels and in college or workplace settings. This does not imply that the use of observation in these situations should not be further developed since other professional training programmes, such as those of doctors and accountants, have traditionally made more extensive use of observation. In Chapter Five Miller-Pietroni has argued that one of the most significant advantages of the use of observation in post-qualifying education and training is the contribution it can make to perspective transformation. This argument could be generalised to other forms of training since the transformation of knowledge, skills and values is an aim of learning at whatever level it takes place. Observation has the potential to play a central role in this process.

In practice settings we have seen examples of this transformation happening in relation to consultancy, the management of practice and inter-professional communication. In these situations, it has been suggested by some contributors to this book that observation provides greater understanding of the breadth of concerns which have to be considered (for example, Kearney's argument for a management style which 'operates at 360 degrees'). Observation has the potential to bring about other qualitative changes, particularly by revealing greater depth in terms of layers of meaning. In Chapter Four the 'ordinary tasks' of residential workers are revealed in all their complexity, illustrating how the intense focus of the observer provides a greater understanding of this complexity. This is because an equal emphasis on addressing process as well as outcomes enables the observer to engage fully with the problems of everyday practice.

Observation and the Wider Context

One of the developments in the application of observation from the individual stance of earlier psychoanalytic perspectives has been the greater emphasis given by our contributors to the interaction between the individual and the wider social and political context. This is particularly relevant to an understanding of the impact of the culture of 'new managerialism' which pervades much of social work in general and community care practice in particular (Sheppard 1995). We have argued earlier in this book that one of the effects of these changes has been to limit the role of professional social work and to challenge the relevance of its skills and values. By contributing to an awareness of the impact of these issues on individuals and organisations, observation enables social workers to construct different forms of 'oppositional space' within which to practice (Comley 1989). Examples of this are the use of the observational role to provide a critique of bureaucratic and hierarchical structures.

Although ideas about consumer power and choice are central to the rhetoric of this changing managerial culture, the reality of the redistribution of influence and the extent of choice for clients has proved to be more elusive (Lewis and Glennerster 1996). Taylor (1996) has suggested that the greater involvement of clients in sharing their experiences and views offers exciting challenges to the educational process. Although there are some imaginative descriptions of these developments (Beresford and Harding 1993; Ramon and Sayce 1993), these approaches have not so far been widely adopted on training programmes.

In the process of looking at the relationship between observation and the wider context we have attempted to describe the theoretical models which influence its development and characteristics. The epistemological roots of the developments which have occurred in the knowledge base of observation have been grouped into the two prevailing approaches which we have called the Narrative and Scientific Models. Ideas about the nature of observation, its values and priorities are not neutral. They are affected by the theories of knowledge which are prevalent at particular times. Currently, social work education is dominated by ideas about competence, which are expressed in the use of observation as a tool of assessment. Reflective practice, based on another influential set of ideas, is regarded as a means of enabling social work values, knowledge and skills to remain central in spite of the ideological context already described. This approach to observation has different characteristics, which pay greater attention to ideas about the nature and use of subjectivity, the construction of meaning and the relationship between the observer and the observed. Several writers have discussed the similarities between and parallel developments in these sets of ideas. For example, Taylor (1996) highlights some of the dilemmas:

> Reflective learning may be conceptualised as a response to postmodernism, as a positive and creative approach to the prospect of living with contingency. The competence approach may also be perceived as a response to postmodernism and the result of a quest for certainty. It is suggested that reflective learning and competence have the potential to be more compatible than is initially apparent. If the competence approach is broadly conceptualised, reflective learning offers the opportunity of providing a crucial component. (p.159)

These are important discussions since, in the main, they are directed towards modifying approaches to competence to ensure that they are more relevant to the realities of social work practice. However, the discussions in Chapter One have shown that these two approaches have developed from different theories of knowledge and, therefore, represent different views of the world. It remains the case that when 'observation' is mentioned without a qualifying context, ideas about its contribution to the collection of 'objective' information are usually inferred.

In this book we have seen how different theoretical approaches underpin the grounding of observation in social work education and practice. Leonard has shown that reflective learning and the competence framework can be used simultaneously by practice teachers and assessors, while the flexible use of psychodynamic ideas has influenced the approaches of Miller-Pietroni, Simmonds and Lewis. Doolan's chapter on observation in family therapy describes a number of ways in which observation is developing from its early systemic thinking while Kearney shows how social construction theory can widen our understanding about the place of observation within management practice.

The Process of Observation

However it is expressed, one of the most significant characteristics of the process of observation is the observer stance. It is clear that whatever theoretical approach underpins the observation, the process involves the observer taking up a position which involves reflection rather than action. This stance is described by Simmonds as putting the 'me in role' in the background and the 'observer me' in the foreground and thus reversing the priorities which are more usual in social work practice. For observation to be effective, it is necessary for the observer to stand outside familiar roles while remaining emotionally active and receptive. This stance is sometimes characterised as primarily an internal process (reflective) and sometimes primarily as an external process (reflexive), though both require the adoption of a critical approach to the material generated by the observation. Miller-Pietroni suggests that reflective observation involves making use of a 'reflective inner space' and avoiding the development of a 'second skin' which protects the observer from the strong and painful feelings which are at the core of social work. These feelings have to be used rather than avoided (Leonard) and Simmonds suggests that they can enable social workers to 'think the unthinkable' about their primary tasks.

This emphasis on the inner world is influenced by psychoanalytic theories. However, as has been discussed in Chapter Two, reflexive practice may have a different emphasis but shares many of the characteristics of reflective practice. There is the same priority given to adopting a critical stance in response to a changing and uncertain world and an emphasis on practitioners developing a 'self monitoring' approach (Sheppard 1995; Taylor 1996). However, reflexivity pays greater attention to an awareness of the ambiguity of relationships in the context of social interaction. This contributes to the development of understanding of the observational process. In these respects, the development of ideas about the stance of the observer are the product of interchanging influences from psychoanalysis and qualitative sociology.

Inevitably, the observational process which has been described is not an easy one since it involves being the receiver of strong feelings without the security of an active role. The discomfort which is frequently acknowledged in the observer role appears to serve a number of important functions. One of these is that it alerts us to the presence of the inequalities of power inherent in the process. Kearney suggests that observation makes people uncomfortable, partly because of lack of familiarity with the process but also because they feel they are making judgements and, therefore, being oppressive. However, there seems to be a consensus that it is essential for the observer to hold on to these uncomfortable feelings and use them as a means of greater understanding (Lewis, Leonard). The impulse to intervene in order to 'make things better' is an important part of this understanding and examples of whether, when or how to intervene have been given by our contributors (Leonard, Simmonds, Miller-Pietroni). In relation to practice teaching, Leonard suggests that the only reason for making an intervention during an observation session in which a client is involved is to prevent risk to that client. In this context, as in all others, the observer has to be alert to processes such as avoidance or action which are possible responses to the feelings generated by observation. Simmonds discusses the struggles of the 'observer me' to make connections, specifically between the observer's active mind and the mind of 'the other' who is being observed. This process is mediated by the impact of the 'raw material' which has to be understood in order to think effectively. Interventions which are part of the consultation processes Simmonds describes are, therefore, the outcome of the interaction between these complex processes of feeling and thought. These arguments highlight the extent to which ideas about the observer stance have shifted as a result of extending the use of observation from the therapeutic environment to a range of different settings. We have argued that the concept of observation is flexible enough to adapt to these changes but what remains constant is a stance which makes use of reflective and reflexive processes in order to make sense of what is being observed before acting on it.

Although I have so far discussed these ideas in relation to an individual observer, there are also important pointers in this book to the use of similar processes in teams or organisations. Doolan has described the place of observation in reflecting teams in family therapy where the therapeutic team uses observation and shared perceptions as a means of understanding the material they observe. Miller-Pietroni argues that observation is a significant element in accessing greater awareness of the potential for rigidity and inflexibility in professional roles. In letting go of some of this defensive and protective rigidity inter-professional communication becomes more effective. Both Kearney and Miller-Pietroni suggest that the use of observational skills can have an impact on the way in which organisations are structured and managed.

The Outcomes of Observation

Observation is both a process and an outcome and the characteristics of the observer stance have an effect on the quality of the resulting learning and practice. The ultimate aim of using observation has to be that it improves the quality of practice to the benefit of service users and clients. There are increasing concerns that the nature of social work is being fundamentally changed in response to ideological imperatives. These concerns relate, among other things, to fears that social work roles and tasks are becoming increasingly routine and residual. The narrative has been lost in the bureaucratic and the whole picture becomes fragmented. Observation appears to be one means of counteracting these tendencies by acting as a 'circuit breaker' (Miller-Pietroni). It puts the focus back on the total picture with all its potential for discomfort and complexity. There is no doubt that these shifts in perception take time, but one of the effects of using observational knowledge and skills seems to be that time is better managed. Even when there is not much time available (or perhaps because there is little time available), it is important not to be precipitated into action. Some of that time, as a resource, has to be allocated to thought rather than action and observation provides a vehicle for doing this.

However, the most significant outcome of the use of observation is its potential contribution to anti-discriminatory and anti-oppressive practice. One characteristic of powerlessness is invisibility and paying greater attention to unequal relationships enables 'the voice of the observed' to be heard (Baldwin 1994). The Equality Model of observation has suggested a number of ways in which the application of a power lens facilitates these developments.

The Equality Model and the Power Lens

One of the characteristics of anti-oppressive observation practice is that it can bring about change. There are as many aspects to that change as there are situations in which observation can be used. Clearly, there are opportunities for individual change in relation to increased opportunities to practise new skills or develop greater awareness of values and knowledge. We have also suggested that observation can result in significantly increased awareness of organisational processes, including the effectiveness of management and supervision. However, we have argued throughout this book that one of the major contributions observation can make to social work practice and education is its contribution to a greater awareness of the impact of power relations at all levels of the process. This begins with an understanding that both the process and outcomes of observation have the potential to be oppressive. Kearney has described this in terms of observation being linked to the forensic aspects of social work, part of an assessment process which can be seen as a means of 'catching people out'. For practitioners, being watched can also feel like being judged and found wanting, particularly when the organisation is experienced as distant, rigid and uncaring. Power differentials are underlined by Kearney's point that it may be all right to observe those in a less powerful position (students or clients) but it does not feel all right to observe colleagues. The first can be justified in terms of good practice while the second feels like intrusion. The most obvious exception to this is in family therapy where the open observation of colleagues is part of the culture in training and in practice (Doolan). Similar feelings will be evoked but they are more openly acknowledged and, therefore, managed more effectively.

Unless the potential for observation to be oppressive is recognised, it becomes far more difficult for practitioners to access the authority and power inherent in their roles and, therefore, use them effectively. Lewis gives an example of this in her description of the training of Approved Social Workers where observation is used as a vehicle for trainees to access their discomfort about their authority and power. This increased understanding enables the trainees to understand more about the nature of their power in role and its impact on mental health practice.

These issues also have an effect on the process of observation where they have frequently not been addressed. We have tried to think about the implications of these concerns by using the metaphor of the power lens to enable us to develop a model of observation which takes account of these realities. In describing the characteristics of the model as it is grounded in practice we have uncovered some of the complexities of the experience of power relations. This includes an understanding of the impact of hierarchical power in both its formal and informal guises and the interaction between power and powerlessness. Formal power in role does not necessarily equate to the subjective experience of power since power and powerlessness can operate simultaneously.

These paradoxes are a central characteristic of personal and professional relationships but inequality becomes more apparent when other aspects of difference are part of the equation. Doolan describes the need to be aware of our own race, gender, class and other differences as they impact on our 'observer self' and interact with the observation process. Leonard has warned of the dangers of making assumptions about the effects of differences in class, race and gender – for example suggesting that these differences have to be discussed openly at the beginning of professional relationships and incorporated into agreements and all other aspects of work. In describing the characteristics of the Equality Model we have suggested that negotiation needs to articulate the nature of power difference and inequality, recognising that openness does not always lead to alterations in the power imbalance. Social work students in training do not have the choice about whether or not to be observed, though within the educational framework there are elements which are open to discussion and negotiation. For clients, the choice of whether or not to be observed during the course of an assessment may not be available, though the conduct of that observation is flexible and has to be discussed.

We have also argued that the skills of giving and receiving feedback have to be further developed. In Chapter Two we have suggested some of the factors which need to be borne in mind in order to devise effective feedback structures and to work in a way which is congruent with social work values. Kearney argues that a systemic approach to working with families uses feedback as a way of responding to observed behaviour. She discusses the ways in which observation and feedback constantly act and react in the process of change. In this context the timing of feedback seems to be important since if it is to be incorporated into change processes, whether in direct practice or education, immediate feedback is necessary. The quality of the tone and texture of feedback involves careful thought, though frequently it seems to be limited by the structure of forms.

In the climate of user and consumer involvement greater attention has to be paid to involving the observed in the process of giving and receiving useful feedback which can be acted upon. As observation takes place in a wider range of social work settings, this development becomes more urgent. Educators and practitioners can find reasons for limiting the extent of the feedback or avoiding it altogether. Sometimes this avoidance is justified in terms of its content (it is too painful) or because, in the context of the observation, it is felt to be inappropriate. Sometimes aspects of difference, such as age or ability, have been used to limit the feedback given after an observation. However, if we are to pursue the idea of the congruence of observation with social work values, we have to continue to work on this issue, however difficult it proves to be. This discussion also suggests that there are further connections which need to be made between the place of feedback, processes of change and power relations.

The Future of Observation in Social Work

The Equality Model of observation is grounded in social work theory and in social work practice. Any attempt to develop a model of observation has to ensure that it is congruent with theory and practice, both of which have to be based on experience. Simmonds suggests that observation can help us to 'construct meaning out of experience' rather than determine meaning prior to experience. In relation to theory building we have seen how, in a postmodern environment, over-arching theories appear to be less useful than those which are flexible enough to respond to particular circumstances. Therefore, theories which illuminate models of observation also have to be grounded in experience (Glaser and Strauss 1967; Guba and Lincoln 1982; Parlett and Hamilton 1981).

However, the process and outcomes of observation are not only the product of knowledge and practice, they also provide opportunities to extend existing boundaries. The Equality Model does this by suggesting ways in which the use of a power lens enables us to recognise the impact of inequalities and develop strategies for bringing about change. It also emphasises the importance of making connections between different dimensions of power – in particular, the impact of structure on emotion. One of the most consistent strands in this book has been the influence observation can have on practice which has become routine and rigidly bureaucratic. While the continued development of reflective and reflexive practice is not a panacea, this book provides numerous examples of their effect on the quality of practice and education. Most significantly, we can see how individual and humanistic values can be retained in an environment which is frequently hostile to such ideas. However, this approach, while important, is not sufficient in a situation of increasing disadvantage and inequality. The development of observation from approaches which have been exclusively individual to those which take account of structural factors will need to continue to take account of these different dimensions. If some of the characteristics of the Equality Model are incorporated into observational practice, it will be even more important for it to become central to social work education and practice.

References

Baldwin, M. (1994) 'Why observe children?' *Social Work Federation 13, 2*, 83.

Beresford, P. and Harding, T. (eds) (1993) *A Challenge to Change. Practical Experiences of Building User-Led Services.* London: National Institute for Social Work.

Comley, T. (1989) 'State social work: a socialist-feminist contribution.' In C. Hallett (ed) *Women and Social Services Departments.* Hemel Hempstead: Harvester Wheatsheaf.

DoH (1988) *Protecting Children: A Guide for Social Workers Undertaking a Comprehensive Assessment.* London: HMSO.

Glaser, M. and Strauss, A. (1967) *The Discovery of Grounded Theory.* Chicago: Aldine.

Guba, E. and Lincoln, Y. (1982) 'Epistemological and methodological bases of naturalistic enquiry.' *Educational, Community and Technical Journal 30*, 4, 233–252.

Lewis, J. and Glennerster, H. (1996) *Implementing the New Community Care.* Buckingham: Open University.

Miles, G. and Bridge, G. (1997) *On the Outside Looking In.* London: CCETSW.

Parlett, M. and Hamilton, D. (1981) 'Evaluation as illumination.' In M. Parlett and G. Dearden (eds) *Introduction to Illuminative Evaluation (Studies in Higher Education).* Guildford: Society for Research into Higher Education.

Ramon, S. and Sayce, L. (1993) 'User participation in mental health: implications for social work education and training.' *Issues in Social Work Education 13*, 2, 53–70.

Rustin, M. (1989) 'Observing infants: reflections on methods.' In L. Miller, M. Rustin, M. Rustin and J. Shuttleworth (eds) *Closely Observed Infants.* London: Duckworth Press.

Sheppard, M. (1995) *Care Management and the New Social Work. A Critical Analysis.* London: Whiting and Birch.

Tanner, K. and Le Riche, P. (1995) '"You see but you do not observe": the art of observation and its application to practice teaching.' *Issues in Social Work Education 15,* 2, 66–80.

Taylor, I. (1996) 'Reflective learning, social work education and practice in the 21st century.' In N. Gould and I. Taylor (eds) *Reflective Learning for Social Work.* Aldershot: Arena.

Trowell, J. and Miles, G. (1991) 'The contribution of observation training to professional developments in social work.' *Journal of Social Work Practice 5,* 1, 51–60.

The Contributors

Moira Doolan is a registered Systemic Psychotherapist and Social Worker who currently works as a Research Therapist at the Institute of Psychiatry, London, and independently as a Systemic Psychotherapist and as a trainer in Family Therapy. She trained as a social worker in her native country, Canada, and has worked in London since 1972. Most of her practice has been as a social worker in child and adult mental health settings, including five years as a member of a specialist team for children who had been sexually abused. She has also worked as a trainer at Kensington Consultation Centre and the Institute of Family Therapy, London.

Patricia Kearney read English at Somerville College, Oxford, where she obtained an MSc in Applied Social Studies in 1975. Since then she has worked in a variety of practice and management posts, with a special interest in family and mental health work. She has worked as a freelance trainer and consultant and as a teacher on the Goldsmiths social work qualifying course. She held a three-year honorary family therapy post at the Maudsley Hospital. Currently, she is a Consultant in the Development Unit at the National Institute for Social Work.

Kate Leonard is a white woman. She has worked in social services offices in London as a generic social worker and senior social worker since 1986. She began working at South Bank University in 1992, first as a Senior Lecturer and Practice Teaching Development Worker, and is currently the Course Director of the Inter-professional Practice Teaching course. She also works as a Guardian *ad litem* and freelance Practice Assessor, Trainer and Consultant.

Pat Le Riche is a Lecturer in Social Work at Goldsmiths College, University of London. Apart from her current work on observation, her main research interests are in ageing and gender, and community care. She has worked in a range of social work agencies, including being a team manager in the statutory sector and a practice teacher in a voluntary community development agency. Teaching experience includes working in a number of different roles for the Open University and lecturing at the University of Kent.

Hazelanne Lewis trained as a social worker in South Africa where she started working in the mental health field. After completing an MA in Community and Primary Care: Towards a Reflective Practice in 1995, she moved into working in training. In 1978 she founded the Stillbirth and Neonatal Death Society (SANDS). She is currently working as a training officer with responsibility for mental health training and is co-ordinator of the Hertfordshire/Barnet Approved Social Work Programme. She is also a Mental Health Act Commissioner.

Marilyn Miller-Pietroni was until recently Principal Lecturer in Primary Health and Community Care at the University of Westminster. Her practice base is Marylebone Health Centre. As a social worker and adult psychotherapist, she taught at the Tavistock Clinic for many years, including on the joint Brunel University MPhil in Social Work. She edited *Right or Privilege?*, a book on post-qualifying training for social workers, is a former editor of the *Journal of Social Work Practice* and, with Jill Spratley, co-authored a report on inter-professional training priorities, *Creative Collaboration*. She is currently leading, with Fiona Bartels-Ellis, the work-based learning programme 'MA in Advanced Social Work'.

John Simmonds is a Senior Lecturer in Social Work at Goldsmiths College, University of London. He is particularly interested in decision making in social work and the use and development of psychodynamic frameworks in social work. Until recently he was the editor of the *Journal of Social Work Practice*.

Karen Tanner is a Lecturer in Social Work at Goldsmiths College, University of London. She has practice experience in child protection and has worked with children suffering from life-threatening illness. She has a particular interest in child observation and is both a teacher and a researcher in this area.

Subject Index

Author Index